RA 1242 .C436 V57 2007
Visser, Melvin J., 1938-
Cold, clear, and deadly

MHCC WITHDRAWN

D0312389

COLD, CLEAR, AND DEADLY

COLD, CLEAR, AND DEADLY

UNRAVELING A TOXIC LEGACY

MELVIN J. VISSER

Michigan State University Press
East Lansing

Copyright © 2007 by Melvin J. Visser

♾ The paper used in this publication meets the minimum requirements of ANSI/NISO
Z39.48-1992 (R 1997) (Permanence of Paper).

Michigan State University Press
East Lansing, Michigan 48823-5245

Printed and bound in the United States of America.

13 12 11 10 09 08 07   1 2 3 4 5 6 7 8 9 10

LIBRARY OF CONGRESS CATALOGING-IN-PUBLICATION DATA
Visser, Melvin J., 1938-
Cold, clear, and deadly : unraveling a toxic legacy / Melvin J. Visser.
p. cm.
Includes bibliographical references and index.
ISBN 978-0-87013-802-7 (hardcover : alk. paper)
1. Organochlorine compounds--Toxicology. 2. Organochlorine
compounds--Environmental aspects. I. Title.
RA1242.C436V57 2007
628.5'2—dc22
2006100328

Cover design by Charles Brock, The DesignWorks Group, www.thedesignworksgroup.com
Cover photography by Steve Gardner, PixelWorks Studios, www.shootpw.com.

For more information, please visit the author's web log at: www.coldclearanddeadly.com

Michigan State University Press is a member of the Green Press Initiative and is
committed to developing and encouraging ecologically responsible publishing practices.
For more information about the Green Press Initiative and the use of recycled paper
in book publishing, please visit www.greenpressinitiative.org.
This book was printed on 100% recycled paper (100% post-consumer content).

Visit Michigan State University Press on the World Wide Web at:

www.msupress.msu.edu

To Gloria

CONTENTS

ACKNOWLEDGMENTS

It has been a privilege to spend a decade in understanding and writing about the source and global transport of the chemical age's most environmentally devastating products. I have been richly blessed with the support of my wife Gloria, who has been patient throughout my extended physical absences while attending a multitude of meetings and conferences or traveling to far stretches of the globe . . . and the mental absences while lost in thought in her presence. She, along with Patrick and Lori, have all been a continuing source of help and encouragement. The "thinking environmentalists" of the Michigan Audubon Society have provided an ongoing sounding board for embryonic ideas, and a group of pastors and friends at Milwood United Methodist Church have given me faith to continue the pursuit of understanding and communication.

Early in my career, dozens of extremely creative chemists and chemical engineers taught me the physical chemical behavior of chemicals in stills, reactors, and columns. Awareness of the effect of chemicals in the environment came from the Great Lakes Regional Corporate Environmental Council (GLRCEC), a group of Canadian and U.S. environmental leaders who wrestled with Great Lakes environmental concerns. Jim Ludwig, Lorraine "Rainy" Campbell, and Fred Brown became special friends and confidants during the years of work in GLRCEC.

Interface with hundreds of scientists and regulators during my industrial career, and later in voluntary efforts, provided an education in environmental research and policy. Of the many helpful and dedicated professionals, G. Tracy Mehan of Michigan's Great Lakes Protection Fund was outstanding in his openness and curiosity.

An up-close Lake Superior education was obtained from Reino Erkkila and his brother Edwin during long hours of fishing for commerce and, when commercial fishing was over, for sport. The unspoiled beauty of the northern Great Lakes and their shorelines was revealed to me through pleasant weeks of cruising Lake Superior and the North Channel of Lake Huron aboard the sailing vessels *Nighthawk* and *Hope* with Captains Sanderson and Carlstrom.

Once the source of persistent organic pollutants in all cold, clear waters of the Northern Hemisphere was found, my support groups encouraged me to write. Engineers are not writers, so another long educational process began. Fortunately, invaluable coaching and assistance were obtained from author Joseph T. Heywood, a former coworker and soccer-coaching partner. Joe's patience with my early efforts, tutelage, and guidance are deeply appreciated. Nature author Emma Pitcher provided her personal Arctic library, proofreading, and excellent critique and commentary based on her many Arctic travels. Neighbor Bob Warner allowed the use of his bookstore as a library.

In later versions, the excellent editorial suggestions of Leslie Lynch removed most of my "technospeak" and helped create an understandable manuscript. Through sharing the manuscript with Michael Boyce of Michigan Audubon, a reconnection with Jim Ludwig and Rainy Campbell led to a rekindling of long-dormant friendships, and eventually to Dave Dempsey of the Michigan Environmental Council.

Dave introduced my efforts to MSU Press, where Martha Bates's initial editorial guidance and suggestions served to remove redundant and superfluous text. The pleasant and productive interactions with MSU Press' Assistant Director/Editor in Chief Julie Loehr, along with Kristine Blakeslee, Annette Tanner, and Julie Reaume resulted in an attractive and polished product focusing on the simple message. . . . Our northern waters may be *Cold, Clear, and Deadly*, but a simple and proven fix is at hand.

It was indeed a privilege to be blessed by the opportunities to research this interesting and devastating subject and an honor to be surrounded by such a diverse array of supportive friends and professionals.

PREFACE

The 1950s, my formative years, were a time of great optimism, trust, and progress. The nation had turned its World War II energies toward consumer satisfaction, bringing us television, plastics, and expressive automobiles. Government, industry, doctors, and the media were trusted . . . opportunity abounded.

Every Sunday afternoon, "Industry on Parade" invaded our living room through a single-channel black-and-white TV, opening exciting windows into the world of powerful, smoke-belching industries. What really hooked me were commercials touting "Better Things for Better Living through Chemistry." Long before my 1955 high-school graduation, I felt that chemicals were my future. After a year of pre-engineering at Grand Rapids, Michigan's junior college, I was certain.

My older brother, George, had served two years in the Korean conflict, was stuck in a dead-end job with IBM, and saw an electrical-engineering degree on the G.I. Bill as his way out. His friend Johnny Van had graduated from the Michigan College of Mining and Technology (Michigan Tech), worked a few years, and wanted to return for an advanced degree in metallurgical engineering. Johnny offered to take us to Houghton, Michigan Tech's home in the far reaches of Michigan's Upper Peninsula. I hoped to transfer there in another year, so I jumped at the opportunity. I'd never been more than a hundred miles north, and was looking forward to crossing the Straits of Mackinac and seeing Lake Superior.

Johnny drove the 250 miles to the tip of Michigan's mitten, where we caught a late ferry across the straits. We team-drove the remaining 275 miles north and west to McLain State Park, on the western side of Lake Superior's Keweenaw Peninsula. Well past midnight, stretched out in a stand of white pine, my road-weary eyes caught glimpses of millions of stars through the lacy pine canopy while I listened to Lake Superior's gentle surf rattle pebbles against the shoreline.

The next time my eyes opened, dawn had erased all but the brightest stars. I crawled out of my sleeping bag and ran down to see her. On the previous night's dark ride, I'd caught glimpses of Lake Superior at Munising and Marquette, but I had to see this greatest of the Great Lakes up close. Our camp was at the west entry of the Portage Canal, a navigable waterway cutting across the Keweenaw Peninsula. Freighters—the 700-foot ore, coal, and grain carriers of the time—used the canal to avoid mid-lake storms when steaming between Wisconsin or Minnesota and the locks to the lower lakes at Sault Ste. Marie (the Soo). I ran down a small dune, across the sandy beach, and carefully picked my way over two hundred feet of stacked granite boulders for a pier's-end view.

She was awesome in the wispy light of a windless dawn. Foot-high steel-grey swells, remnants of an invisible storm somewhere on her 37,000 square miles, slunk in from the distant horizon and gently broke at her shore. Offshore, white-trimmed ripples dancing along the swells were turning dusky rose, reflecting a sunrise-tinted strip of cirrus. It was hard to believe this calm giant had sunk thousands of ships.

I felt comfortably insignificant and, for a cocky eighteen-year-old, humble in the presence of the world's largest body of fresh water—larger than the other Great Lakes combined, plus three more volumes of Lake Erie. If spilled, she could cover the continental United States with six feet of water. Yet, she was hurting. Opening a commercial route to the sea allowed sea lampreys to enter her waters. She had no defense against these foreigners, and the lampreys were sucking the vital juices from her most valuable crop, the tasty northern varieties of lake trout. She'd supplied regional markets with millions of pounds per year, but now her lamprey-damaged breeders were incapable of reproducing. Her eagles and cormorants had abandoned her, and she was beginning to feel sick. She didn't seem to be able to support life as she had in years past.

I scanned her surface without knowledge of the serene giant's problems. Water and sky met in a distant curved line, unblemished by the ever-present horizon-blotting haze of the lesser Great Lakes. When I put my hand into the water to pick up some of the colorful pebbles, the cold penetrated my wrist like a knife. The clearness of the water allowed a view of rocks well out of my reach. Lake Superior seemed so clean, so pure. I hoped to get to know her better. My falling in love with a lake was interrupted by three beeps from a distant car horn. I rushed back to join George and Johnny. Maybe I'd come back in the fall.

I did return, graduated from Michigan Tech, and enjoyed a twenty-year career encompassing all the engineering and chemistry challenges of medicinal chemical and antibiotic manufacture at the Upjohn Company in Kalamazoo, Michigan. This career was followed by sixteen years of responsibility for environmental compliance and remediation. Cleaning up the mess I created, my friends say.

Process research and manufacturing experience provided me with comprehensive training in the behavior of chemicals as they were created in reactors, carefully separated from complex reaction mixtures and purified to exacting standards. The environmental experience taught me how released or discarded chemicals entered the air, water, and wildlife of the Great Lakes region.

At the time of my formal education, it was believed that nature rapidly degraded all chemicals released into the environment. Modern chemistry challenged nature, and chemicals began showing up in dangerous levels in groundwater, rivers, lakes, and oceans. My manufacturing and environmental careers schooled me well in both the generation and fate of chemicals, but one phenomenon I could not understand was the refusal of banned chemicals to leave Lake Superior.

During my last years of employment, I became obsessed with these recalcitrant chemicals and sought to learn their source, follow their movement though the environment, and understand their persistence. Early retirement in 1995 allowed time to search for the deadly secrets of cold, clear waters through volunteer efforts with federal and state agencies, international meetings, and travel to the Arctic.

The source, transport, fate, and effect of the banned chlorinated organic chemicals known as "dirty-dozen persistent organic pollutants" (POPs) has unfolded like a mystery novel, with chemicals as characters. People, of course, control the chemicals, and at times relationships between politics, regulation, science, and global business lead to situations that would be comical if they were not so tragic. Can you imagine one group of experts telling people to eat food so toxic that another group calls it hazardous waste? Experts from the same country? A "developed" country? Can you imagine the most toxic chemical in Great Lakes fish not being included in fish-eating advisories?

Most progress in understanding requires relinquishment of tightly held beliefs. Early in my career, I knew that nonvolatile chemicals such as PCBs and DDT could not move from a use or disposal point to the remote and pristine Lake Superior. If a few molecules could get there, how could they possibly pollute such a large body of water to levels that would affect wildlife? The eagles and cormorants might have disappeared, but not because of some nonvolatile chemical. There had to be another reason—maybe biological. In later, humbling interactions with environmentalists, I learned that everything I knew should be questioned.

Scores of people have helped me in my journey of learning. Most of their names have been changed to protect the innocent and the guilty. When a person cannot be disguised because of their actions or position, his/her full name will be given. At times, a single name is used, and the person is a generic representation of his/her position or organization and not to be confused with any person, living or dead.

ABBREVIATIONS

AMAP	Arctic Monitoring and Assessment Programme
ATSDR	Agency for Toxic Substance and Disease Registry
CFCs	chlorofluorocarbons
CINE	Center for Indigenous Peoples' Nutrition and Environment
DDT	dichloro-diphenyl-trichloroethane
DEQ	Department of Environmental Quality
DEW Line	Distant Early Warning Line
DNR	Department of Natural Resources
F&W	Federal Fish and Wildlife Service
FDA	Food and Drug Administration
GLRCEC	Great Lakes Regional Corporate Environmental Council
HCBs	hexachlorobenzenes
HCH	hexachlorocyclohexane
IADN	Integrated Atmospheric Deposition Network
ICC	Inuit Circumpolar Conference
IJC	International Joint Commission
MCC	Michigan Chemical Council
NAFTA	North American Free Trade Agreement
NGO	non-governmental organization
PCBs	polychlorinated biphenyls
POPs	persistent organic pollutants
ppb	parts per billion
ppm	parts per million
SAO	Settlement Administrative Officer
SOLEC	State of the Lakes Ecosystem Conference
TDI	Tolerable Daily Intake
TMDL	Total Maximum Daily Load
TRI	Toxics Reduction Inventory
UNEP	United Nations Environmental Programme
USEPA	United States Environmental Protection Agency
VOCs	Volatile Organic Compounds

ENVIRONMENTAL EXPOSURE: 1980–1991

LEAVING TIN CITY: SEPTEMBER 1980, THE UPJOHN COMPANY, PORTAGE, MICHIGAN

"Ward wants to talk to you," Bob said as I stood to leave our weekly updating session. Robert A. Donia, Ph.D., vice president for Chemical Operations and my current boss, was an ingenious process chemist and skilled manager. Bob had been a technical consultant, advisor, mentor, and friend during my entire career. The seriousness of his tone stopped me in my tracks. "He has something to offer you."

"What?" I asked, wondering what the Engineering and Maintenance vice president would want with me. I had worked for Ward for the first year of my career and could not relate to the classical engineering efforts of designing, constructing, and maintaining. I loved chemical processes, not hardware.

"I'll let him tell you what," Bob continued, "but he definitely needs someone with your experience. I don't want to see you go, but for your sake, I'd recommend you call him."

While waiting to meet with Ward, I reflected back on the past twenty years. Landing a chemical-processing job at The Upjohn Company in 1959 was a chemical engineer's equivalent of a programmer joining Microsoft as Windows became commercial, or being with Cisco Systems as Internet use skyrocketed.

During World War II, Upjohn was a family-owned pharmaceutical packager and a manufacturer of bulk penicillin. By the mid-1950s, Upjohn scientists had developed several outstanding antibiotics, along with the fermentation technology needed to make large quantities at low cost. In a breakthrough discovery, Upjohn's researchers chemically and biologically converted soybean-processing residues to corticosteroids, allowing commercial manufacture of a host of miracle drugs. Upjohn was on the cutting edge of medicinal chemical technology, and ripe for explosive growth.

Corrugated-metal construction shacks, leftover buildings from the creation of a gigantic pharmaceutical plant in suburban Kalamazoo, were fitted with reactors, distillation units, and crystallizers to make progesterone and cortisone. "Tin City" expanded rapidly, and by 1980 it was a sprawling complex that included modern brick-and-mortar chemical plants, research towers, and a complex of fermentation vessels the size of grain silos.

Pharmaceutical manufacturing is a straightforward and clean operation. Active ingredients, such as those supplied from Tin City, are formulated into tablets, capsules, sprays, fluids, ointments, or sterile solutions for injection. The compounded product is packaged, labeled, boxed, and shipped. There are no chemical reactions and little waste.

Tin City operations are on the other end of the spectrum. Antibiotics are made by nurturing a broth containing tons of sugars, carbohydrates, proteins, and salts for days or weeks to produce a few pounds of purified product and tons of waste. Some of the corticosteroids required a dozen and a half chemical steps to go from raw material to product—chemistry requiring exotic and hazardous reactants, and tank cars of organic solvents.

In chemistry, not all molecules of a starting material follow the desired path to product. Research chemists feel they understand a process if four out of five molecules go from starting material to desired product, an 80 percent yield. The impurities created along with the desired product are a spectrum of chemicals that must be removed through chemical-engineering operations such as distillation, extraction, crystallization, ion exchange, adsorption, or chromatography. Every operation loses yield and creates waste. If it took eighteen 80 percent–yield chemical steps to produce a product, the overall yield would be 1.8 percent. Think of the waste! You have to start with 50 pounds of starting material to get a pound of product . . . assuming you can get all yields to 80 percent.

Upjohn did think of the costly waste. They hired the best process organic chemists and engineers in the country to study, improve, and short-circuit the long routes to products. I was thrilled to be a part of Upjohn's process-improvement team. Through laboratory and pilot-plant experimentation, we raised yields while improving quality and slashing costs. I enjoyed all aspects of chemical operations. How could Ward tempt me away?

Ward greeted me like the old friend he was and unfolded his reorganization plans. He wanted me to head up a division that included Environmental Affairs. Someone with a process background was needed because Engineering had gotten "a little behind" in environmental compliance.

I had difficulty understanding how we could be behind. We had eliminated chemicals suspected of causing cancer, partnered with the city to build one of the finest wastewater treatment plants in the nation, and spent millions on a deepwell to dispose of water contaminated with traces of salts and solvents. I had been personally involved with installing dozens of state-of-the-art vacuum pumps to keep volatile organic compounds (VOCs) out of the air. An ultra-high-temperature rotary waste-disposal kiln was under construction to destroy our research animals, medical waste, and spent solvents (solvents too contaminated to upgrade by distillation and reuse.) What more could we do?

I was soon to learn that the beauty of my beloved "Tin City," that paradise of efficient chemistry and supplier of miracle-producing corticosteroids and antibiotics to the world, was in the eye of the beholder. Others saw her differently.

TO VENUS: 1980–

A few surprises are expected with any job change, but entering the world of environmental compliance was unreal. It was like moving from Mars to Venus. In my Martian world of chemical manufacturing, nature's laws were studied to gain understanding, and then applied to supply a needed product, make money, and stay in business. The rules of chemistry and physics never changed.

The Venusian's laws and rules of environmental compliance were created by politicians and bureaucrats in adversarial forums, pitting the environmental activist's pursuit of the ideal against industry's demand for the economical. Individual industrial players contributed to the chaos by fighting for their own special treatments. The resulting regulations were difficult to understand, impossible to follow, and constantly changing. When the regulations didn't change, the interpretation of them did. I was in another world.

On leaving the orderly Martian world of chemical manufacture, I was immediately faced with a set of Venusian problems. We were installing a natural-gas-fired boiler to supplement our four coal boilers. Natural gas, with fuel-oil backup, was the fuel of choice because it was near impossible to obtain environmental permits for a small industrial coal-fired boiler. While we were designing and constructing, President Carter's Department of Energy was writing regulations requiring new boilers to burn coal. Our facility was declared "non-existing" because it was not commissioned before the rules were finalized. We couldn't start it up! Then there was the waste-disposal kiln.

In a proactive effort, we replaced an inefficient incinerator with an ultramodern rotary kiln capable of achieving operating temperatures and retention times guaranteed to destroy all waste while minimizing dioxin emissions. Dioxin is created in all fires, but the regulators were pressured to eliminate any industrially generated dioxin. Our tests, using the most sensitive analytical procedures available, could not detect dioxin. When the permit was to be signed, the dioxin requirement was one-tenth of the current limit of detection. We were ordered to meet limits to be defined by an assay under development by a consortium of universities. Would detection of a single molecule of dioxin shut down this state-of-the-art facility?

I'd thought of Superfund as money collected from chemical companies to clean up abandoned dumps, but soon found it to be a fund to hire lawyers to force corporations to clean up dumps. My most memorable Superfund settlement was one to clean up an abandoned recycling and disposal site in Indiana. The EPA examined the defunct facility's records, determined the contribution of waste by all of its customers, and invited three hundred companies to participate in a rapid settlement. Once in a closed room, the corporations could see their records and decide on the spot to pay EPA's assessment of cost . . . or face triple the amount. The EPA-supplied records indicated that we shipped 1,200 drums to the site and they shipped 1,050 drums to us. It was clear that they refined and returned solvent to us, but our share of the cleanup was determined by adding 1,200 and 1,050. No questions allowed, just pay up. We didn't.

"This environmental stuff is nuts," I screamed at Bill, an independent environmental attorney our legal department hired to help me at the Indiana party. "How many of these sites are you working on for us?"

"Eight," he said, blowing a puff of pipe smoke out the car window, "and there's bound to be at least that many waiting in the wings."

"And that's not all," I said, and went on and on about how environmental regulations and an impossible permitting process were keeping us from making new chemicals and even thwarting efforts to improve emission controls. "These laws don't make sense," I concluded. "They're unreal."

Bill was one of Michigan's best environmental attorneys and a patient listener. "Laws and regulations are like children," Bill said, after I ran out of air. "It takes time for them to mature. Laws were needed to clean up Lake Erie, air too toxic to breathe, and dumps that pollute groundwater. History will judge them well, but for now we're in for a bumpy ride."

Lucky me, I thought—just in time for the bumps. I might as well get some advice from this guy while I've got him captive. "From what you know of our company, what do you see as our biggest bump?" I asked.

"Air permits," he said. "I don't know how you've managed to operate with unpermitted chemical processes."

Bill was right: it wasn't long before I was summoned to the Michigan Department of Natural Resources, informed of their concern, threatened with criminal action, and told of the necessity for permitting all new operations or operational changes. What I had perceived from Mars as necessary and appropriate emissions of unobtrusive solvents was seen from Venus as unnecessary and vile pollution. Perhaps the Venusians were right, because a few years later we would be identified as the largest emitter of smog-producing volatile organic compounds (VOCs) in the state. We'd also be tabbed as the biggest discharger of hazardous materials to the state's surface waters, something we'll get into later.

Bill was also right about the reality of the laws. I had to realize that they were here to stay, and we would continue to be caught in difficult situations as we and the laws matured. It was my responsibility to manage those situations to the best of my ability. I got our legal department to hire Bill, and I became personally involved in state-level environmental committees of manufacturing associations to ensure our understanding of all existing laws.

The transition from Mars to Venus was difficult, and I remained annoyed with the lack of scientific input into the political process of environmental compliance. Fortunately, I became associated with a group of equally frustrated leaders of major Great Lakes industrial and environmental organizations.

THE GLRCEC: 1982–

While my industrial cohorts and I complained about our impeded competitive capability, environmental activists decried the lack of enforcement of newly established regulations and the slow progress of instituting programs under newly enacted federal laws. To "take over" responsibility for a federal program, states had to pass a law that was equivalent to or stricter than the federal law, then promulgate rules and regulations under the enabling state law. This process required multiple public hearings, sessions that frequently degenerated into emotional shouting matches as activists vented their rage and industries resisted change.

A relentless flow of federal laws to protect and preserve air and water, prevent harm from chemical exposure, and address past, present, and future waste disposal were working their way through the system. State environmental agencies were inundated with the regulatory development effort, permit processing, and enforcement of the growing set of regulations. Permitting and enforcement suffered, much to the dissatisfaction of industry and environmentalists.

Michigan's Department of Natural Resources (DNR) director took a creative approach to addressing adversarial confrontation and complaint: he invited state industry and environmental leadership to a week-long retreat at a conference center located in a stand of northern white pine. Our public-relations manager attended, and returned amazed by the commonality he found between industrialists and activists. He, a power-company executive, a public-relations representative from Dow Chemical, the executive director of the Michigan Audubon Society, and two Great Lakes environmental leaders saw real value in environmentalists and industry leaders meeting under nonadversarial conditions. They desired to continue the forum, expanding it to leadership from the entire Great Lakes Basin. Michigan Audubon was willing to serve as a coordinator, the Mott Foundation and others would provide initial funding, and oh, by the way, they wanted me to cochair this unique venture.

I wondered what I was getting into, but accepted the challenge. It couldn't make things worse.

The following years of monthly meetings and projects with the Great Lakes Regional Corporate Environmental Council (GLRCEC) were educational beyond belief. Our membership was limited to leaders in industry or environmental groups in the states and provinces bordering the Great Lakes, and our discussions were not released except in position papers approved by all GLRCEC members. After a couple of tentative meetings, ideas and opinions flowed easily between the members as we gained trust and learned from each other.

A frequent GLRCEC discussion topic was the disappearance and deformation of Great Lakes eagles and cormorants. The environmentalists suspected chemicals and were honing in on PCBs and DDT.

PCBs and DDT were not of concern to the GLRCEC industrial members. How could already banned and controlled chemicals affect our lives? Personally, I couldn't believe that PCBs and DDT were the culprits. How could they get from an ancient use or disposal site to Lake Superior? The environmentalists suspected that some of the birds brought the chemicals back from their wintering in or near countries that hadn't banned them. I was comfortable believing that banned chemicals were not the cause of wildlife's problems and didn't search for an explanation.

I gladly accepted Michigan Audubon's invitation to a symposium meant to scientifically prove the cause for loss of eagles, cormorants, and other birds from the Great Lakes. I hoped for enlightenment, but didn't realize that attendance would forever change my viewpoint regarding POPs.

MY EPIPHANY: FRIDAY, 27 SEPTEMBER 1991, TRAVERSE CITY, MICHIGAN

If an epiphany is defined as "a sudden manifestation or perception of the essential nature or meaning of something," the Audubon symposium was delivering one in slow motion. No succinct phrases from a burning bush, or bolt of lightning to knock me to my knees—simply a series of thirty-minute scientific presentations hammering at me, unraveling a lifetime of comfortable beliefs. My head pounded as neurons raced to delete firmly held concepts and reprogram for new facts—heretofore heresy—about chemicals and Great Lakes wildlife.

Traces of POPs in Great Lakes water—water you can freely drink without fear of health effects—are magnified to life-destroying levels as they assimilate into microorganisms and bioaccumulate up the food chain. POPs enter the fat of all species. When a POPs-contaminated critter becomes prey, its POPs accumulate in the predator's fat, waiting for that predator's turn to become prey. At each step, POPs concentration can be magnified a hundred-fold or more. The resulting eagle's egg contains POPs at tens of thousands of times the concentration in the water supporting the eagle's food supply.

This was deeply disturbing news: chemicals dispersed into the environment could concentrate to harmful levels in wildlife through the natural process of bioaccumulation. Dilution was not the solution to POPs pollution!

It was painful to realize that the reason for the demise of cormorants and eagles was indeed chemical, even if I wasn't involved in the manufacture or use of the causative chemicals.

To ease the pain, I employed an escape mechanism I'd acquired during a thirty-year industrial career. I tuned out the presenters' unrelenting flow of mind-bending input and turned to peaceful thoughts of Lake Superior. Lake Superior, the cold killer who "never gives up her dead," may seem a strange place to find peace, but memories of spectacular times on her shores and waters beckon me back in times of stress. I reminisced about a canoe trip with my young son along the Keweenaw Peninsula's uninhabited, rugged shoreline. The next replay was along what is now the Pictured Rocks National Lakeshore east of Munising. On a calm fall day, Patrick and I poked the well-dented and creased aluminum canoe into surf-carved caves at the base of massive red sandstone cliffs, then paddled east past Castle Falls and along the powdery white sand of Twelve Mile Beach. Weather stopped us from rounding Au Sable point, so we beached and walked up to the old lighthouse. The memory of the breathtaking beauty of Au Sable dunes across the bay was successfully tuning out the speaker currently addressing Michigan Audubon Society's "The Cause/Effect Linkages II" symposium.

I thought about my last canoe trip in May 1989, a five-day venture along the offshore islets and coves of Lake Superior's Isle Royale to celebrate my daughter's graduation from Michigan Tech. Lori, her fiancé, and I camped alongside a snow bank, feeling like we were in a zoo as the wood ducks, foxes, and rabbits came to see the year's first visitors and the moose stood for photo opportunities.

Dr. James Ludwig, GLRCEC member, past Michigan Audubon president, and cochair of the symposium, stirred beside me and nodded knowingly when I brought my attention back from the memorable canoe trips. He had interpreted my meditational respite as rapt attention and assent to the truths being presented. Not that I disagreed; I just didn't need it pounded in any deeper. My thoughts went back to the fall that I started my chemical-engineering education at Michigan Tech.

I quickly fell in love with the school, the area, and on first sight, Gloria—a cheerleader from Suomi College, the Finnish Lutheran seminary and community college across the lake. If the route to a man's heart is through his stomach, Gloria had an express ticket. Her father's small IGA store boasted an outstanding butcher. The family lived above the IGA, and Friday night's broiled choice steak with garlic bread was the second-finest eating I'd ever experienced. The best was the fresh lake trout her mother's brothers would bring in from their commercial operation. Gloria's uncles were commercial fishermen . . . could I go on the lake with them? Yes! Gloria and I, and her family, were married after my junior year.

Gloria's maternal grandfather emigrated from Finland in 1900 and worked the copper mines long enough to purchase a long-line fishing boat. He homesteaded at the mouth of Traverse River, near the Keweenaw/Houghton county border on Keweenaw Bay, and raised two sons and two daughters. The girls left their isolated home in their teens, going to Detroit for work, then returned to raise their own families. The boys, Reino and Edwin, stayed in the fishing business and between them raised six daughters, lamenting the lack of progeny to propagate the business. After the sea lampreys decimated the lake trout, there was little chance for a continuing business.

The Erkkila brothers geared up for chubs and herring. Herring came into their Keweenaw Bay spawning grounds in November, while chubs, a fatter fish and fantastic eating when smoked, could be found at any time. I joined my new uncles on the boat whenever I could. A favorite trip was toward Keweenaw Point for trout, with a few premium chubs as a side product.

I'd enjoy a day of fishing and storytelling, then "drive" the boat home while they cleaned a hundred select chubs. They'd salt the chubs overnight in a giant crock, "with a little sugar in the water," and load them onto racks in the smokehouse early the next morning. I'd tend the smoker, keeping it smoldering with freshly peeled and split sugar-plum branches, until they returned from the day's fishing. We'd unload their catch, and Reino would finish cooking the fish with a charge of dried hard maple.

That was the fun fishing—in Novembers, I hired on as a "herring choker." You grip a slippery herring by the throat, remove gill-net strings from its mouth and gills, and then squeeze it through the mesh and onto the floor. By the end of the haul, you're up to your waist in five tons of fish and get to shovel them into boxes. At the dock, the catch is off-loaded to an awaiting truck. The twenty bucks a day was appreciated and needed, but more than that, it provided motivation to study.

During moderate catches, there was time for talk. Reino told of the cormorants that once inhabited Lake Superior. I hadn't known of cormorants other than from geography books showing the Chinese practice of using birds to catch fish.

"Where are they now?" I asked.

"Went away," he answered with a faraway look in his eyes.

"Did you have eagles?" I asked.

"When we were kids, they nested at Big Louie's Point," Edwin said.

"Did they go away too?" I asked.

"Greedy loggers cut their nesting trees down," Reino said.

I was jolted from memories of this conversation by the speaker's concluding statement: "It is beyond a shadow of doubt that bald eagle reproductive impairment in the Great Lakes Basin is due to organochlorine contamination."

"Went away," I thought. They sure did; they couldn't reproduce. But how did the PCBs and DDT reach Lake Superior and contaminate its tremendous volumes of water? There were no POPs-polluting industries or significant agricultural complexes in the Lake Superior basin!

Earlier presentations had introduced the forensic-science approach to understanding the toxicology of the Great Lakes. Cold, hard, irrefutable evidence that chlorinated organic chemicals had caused a severe reduction in or the complete demise of trout, cormorant, gull, tern, and mink populations was presented with a vengeance.

"You're hammering this pretty hard," I said to Dr. Jim Ludwig, the symposium cochair, still sitting beside me and enjoying my agony. Jim was an outstanding field biologist and a key researcher in the tern and cormorant studies. He kept a cross-beaked, double-crested cormorant named Cosmos in a swimming pool and paraded him out for activist functions. I met Jim through the Great Lakes Regional Corporate Environmental Council, and despite being from opposite sides of the chemical spectrum, we grew to respect each other's views and worked together on environmental-restoration projects. Jim had assessed me as "ready" to hear the message of this conference and extended a personal invitation I couldn't refuse. I was the only industry person present.

"Had to have absolute proof of causality," Jim said. "Our first symposium, two and a half years ago, got clobbered for lack of exacting scientific proof. Think we have it?"

"In spades," I said.

"Always thought you were salvageable," Jim said, and left to facilitate a panel discussion.

I took a break; walked around the conference center's golf course; watched the sun sink over yellow, orange, and red-tinged hills across the bay; and breathed the fresh, crisp fall air. A brisk walk cleared my thoughts and in turn raised a level of doubt about the cause of Great Lakes contamination. Were chemicals really causing the wildlife destruction? Did they make the eagles and cormorants "go away?" Or had I been duped into believing so by a mass action of misguided scientists bent upon destroying industry—the very industry that fed and clothed them, transported them to conferences, and supplied them with laboratories, chemicals, and equipment for their work?

I walked faster and replayed the presentations of the day. I had not been duped. The presenters were well-respected, leading university scientists of impeccable academic and moral standards. DDT, PCBs, and other "hard" pesticides were doing the damage, but why were they still in the environment? Some had been banned for more than a decade—certainly enough time for them to be captured in sediments, attacked by ozone or other powerful atmospheric chemicals, or metabolized by microbes and other life forms.

Yesterday's belief was that anything made a decade ago was now decomposed or on its way to becoming a sedimentary rock of the next geological age. Now, chemicals I'd written off as gone were still interfering with Great Lakes wildlife reproduction. What about the human ingestion of POPs? Was that a problem? I didn't like this epiphany.

HUMAN EFFECTS: FRIDAY, 27 SEPTEMBER 1991

I felt uneasy, like a new convert among confident elders of a strange religion, as Gloria and I grazed on snacks at Michigan Audubon's evening reception. The environmental scientists and activists were aglow with success and eager to expand the horizons of forensic environmental science, to find chemical causes for all manner of human and wildlife ills, and to ban still more chemicals. As the environmental-compliance executive for the largest emitter of toxic air pollutants in the state, I was definitely behind the lines, deep into enemy territory. It was not the place to argue. We'd enjoy the reception for a polite moment and let them enjoy their success.

Jim Ludwig introduced Theo Colburn, his symposium cochair—a toxicologist and senior fellow of the World Wildlife Fund. Theo's research implicated PCBs and other "dioxin-like" compounds as hormone mimickers and endocrine disrupters leading to reproductive problems and birth defects in humans and wildlife. Theo and Jim were presenting "The Human Cancer Paradigm Reviewed: An Inadequate Means to Protect Piscivorous Great Lakes Wildlife and Humans" in the next afternoon's session. I hated to think of what that implied. In the morning session chaired by Theo Colburn, she'd teased us with an implication that her research results harbored something for the men in the audience. It was well known that she was relating a decrease in sperm count to the presence of PCB and similar compounds in the environment, but she was thought to be far from proving a cause/effect linkage. Their presentation would certainly point out the need to control chemicals . . . more chemicals, and to ridiculously low levels. I didn't want to hear it.

"Will you be around for our presentation?" Jim asked after we'd parted from Theo's company.

"I'll have to read it; we have to be home for the evening," I fibbed. "But I'd like to hear the Jacobsens in the morning."

Drs. Joseph and Sandra Jacobsen of the Department of Psychology at Wayne State University in Detroit were studying the effect of mothers' consumption of Lake Michigan fish on the health and development of their children. Within three groups consuming none, a moderate amount, or a large amount of Lake Michigan fish, several of the forty physical and psychological measurements they could perform on babies indicated negative effects of fish consumption. Publication of their results brought a flurry of defensive responses from industry. Study design, the small number of women involved, and the difficulty of measuring responses in babies were questioned. The Jacobsens would report on follow-up measurements on the children as four-year-olds, and preliminary results of tests on the now eleven-year-olds.

"The Jacobsens are right over there," Jim said. "I'll introduce you."

We enjoyed a few moments with Sandra and Joseph Jacobsen before Gloria and I departed for the evening. The Jacobsens could not divulge any study results, but their faces told me to expect scientific vindication in the morning. I wasn't disappointed. The Jacobsens' updated study confirmed that among other things, the children of mothers exposed to higher levels of Lake Michigan fish suffered attention deficit disorder, had poorer motor skills, and were significantly behind in reading and math skills.

"Will any of your staff be attending the IJC meeting?" Jim asked as I was leaving.

"Jack, my new environmental manager," I said. "He's curious about the IJC's interest in Pollution Prevention."

The International Joint Commission (IJC), a nonregulatory U.S./Canadian advisory agency created in the early 1900s to advise on water issues along the shared 3,000-mile border, was meeting the next day. In the mid-1970s, the IJC added water quality to its charter, and the 1989 biennial meeting was picketed by activists insisting that the IJC champion zero discharge of toxic persistent chemicals.

As chair of the Public Affairs committee of the Michigan Chemical Council (MCC) and involved in state lobbying efforts, I was aware of the IJC and their bent to cater to the environmental activist community's need for a forum. However, MCC's political professionals said the IJC was only an advisory body, not a regulating authority, and couldn't hurt us. I hadn't considered the meeting as something worth attending.

"Could be an interesting meeting for Jack," Jim said. "The environmentalists are considering some creative approaches."

From his smug look, I should have realized something big was brewing. An unprecedented alliance of environmental organizations was coming together to fry something other than fish. The chemical industry—my industry—was their target, and they were formulating a unique weapon: the chlorine bomb!

THE CHLORINE WAR, 1991–1993

THE ACTIVISTS: SEPTEMBER 1991, TRAVERSE CITY, MICHIGAN

Traverse City's transformation from a laid-back resort town to a sprawling development of condos, lakeshore mansions, and strip malls had threatened the water quality of its bays and obliterated scenic orchards and vineyards. The very reasons for its attractiveness were being lost to its development. A core of environmentally concerned citizens questioned the definition of fast growth as progress and developed an outstanding program for preserving scenic spaces, controlling sprawl, and protecting the watershed. Area environmentalists were seasoned in conflict and ready to rise to bigger challenges when the IJC came to town.

It may have taken a scientific symposium for me to understand bioaccumulation of POPs as the source of Great Lakes wildlife demise, but environmental activists were already certain of the relationship between chemicals in the environment and wildlife reproductivity. The International Joint Commission's (IJC) 1989 biennial meeting in Hamilton, Ontario, was stormed by a group of three hundred activists demanding zero discharge.

When the International Joint Commission came to Traverse City, the local activists were well organized and prepared to rally. A coalition of thirteen U.S., Canadian, Great Lakes, and First Nations environmental groups invited everyone to participate in five days of workshops, parades, a demonstration at the nearby Big Rock Nuclear Power Plant, concerts, and a Zero Discharge Rally.

Environmentalists were frustrated by the continuing presence of damaging quantities of POPs in wildlife. Initially, the levels of these chemicals fell rapidly, raising optimism for the return of the eagles and cormorants, and the lifting of fish-eating advisories. After a few short years of declining POPs levels, progress virtually ceased. Eagles returned and attempted to breed on the shorelines of the Great Lakes, but their eggs broke or didn't hatch. When eggs hatched, the resulting chicks were club-footed or cross-beaked. It was time to insist upon complete cessation of industry's POPs discharges. Zero! Now!

The IJC meeting would provide an excellent forum for promoting zero discharge. IJC commissioners had assumed the role of protector of Great Lakes water quality and announced "zero discharge intentions" for both the United States and Canada. Responsible officials of federal, state, and provincial governments would be in attendance to report progress.

Environmental activists were at their wit's end. If the EPA could revive a dead Lake Erie and NASA could put a man on the moon, why couldn't the IJC and their governments remove toxic persistent bioaccumulative chemicals from the Great Lakes? The answer was painfully obvious to the environmentalists: governments were too soft on industry.

The IJC was offering Pollution Prevention as a new approach. Pollution Prevention was a buzzword meaning to prevent pollution by designing pollutants out of a process. Industry called it "process redesign": a fresh look at the overall process, with minimization of waste as an up-front objective instead of an afterthought. Remarkable examples of cost and environmental savings had attracted many industries to the technique.

Pollution Prevention could reduce waste, but how could the banned POPs disappear by the reduction of emissions of solvents and cleaning chemicals? There were no POPs used in industry; they were banned. Industry bought into Pollution Prevention, but not as a POPs-reduction solution. The few industrial public-relations minions sent to monitor IJC's proceedings hoped to spend most of their time at the Jack Nicklaus–designed golf course instead of listening to environmentalists pushing an impossible objective.

Industry was caught golfing as the activists overwhelmed the meeting and focused the IJC's efforts on a creative approach—an industry-devastating approach—to zero discharge.

THE CHLORINE BOMB: SATURDAY, 28 SEPTEMBER 1991

The late Saturday-afternoon call I received from Jack, my new Environmental Affairs manager attending the IJC meeting, launched a new dimension to the Pollution Prevention argument.

"Glad to catch you, boss. Did you hear what happened here?" Jack asked, sounding as if he'd run a mile for the phone.

"The protest at the Big Rock Nuclear Plant made the local TV news and the newspapers covered the activists' gathering and concert," I said. "Anything else happening?"

"They recommended banning chlorine," Jack said.

"What?" I said, laughing incredulously. "A chemical element cannot be banned."

"The activists recommended it," Jack said, sounding confident of the fact that a small group of activists in Traverse City could erase an element from the periodic table.

"Go slow," I said. "What exactly is it they recommended?"

"There was a lot of shouting and parading, but it boiled down to zero use of chlorine in the Great Lakes Basin," Jack said. "A total ban. Zero. Nothing."

"No drinking-water chlorination?!" I shouted, thinking of the millions of potential deaths from drinking untreated water.

"Chlorinating water produces carcinogens," Jack said.

"I suppose they're not going to chlorinate wastewater-treatment-plant effluents to control pathogenic discharges either," I said.

"Right," Jack said. "The treatment process creates chlorinated organics that are toxic to the fish in the receiving waters."

I knew that. It was proven years ago, but a pathogen-free outfall was thought to be a superior option for streams and rivers. Chlorine use was carefully controlled to avoid fish casualties.

"I hope you stood up and got an exemption for chlorine use in the manufacture of pharmaceutical chemicals," I said, "or we don't have a job!"

"Nobody from industry stood up," Jack said. "There was this overwhelming stacking of the deck by the activists and this guy Commoner—"

"Barry Commoner was there?!" I shouted.

"You know him?" Jack asked.

"Know of him," I said. "He's the guy who took the lead out of gasol. . . ." My voice trailed off and I went numb as the Pollution Prevention connection sunk in.

Barry Commoner was the activist who'd led the fight against airborne lead. The EPA was reducing the amount of lead allowed in gasoline, and industry fought them through every step of a slow and painful process. Dr. Commoner successfully convinced the EPA that the only way to reduce lead in the air was to eliminate lead from gasoline. Are you familiar with unleaded gasoline?

Jack filled in the details. Barry Commoner took the reins and led the flock through a straight line of impeccable logic—logic that paralleled the successful removal of lead from gasoline to assure clean air.

It would take years to evaluate the 11,000 chlorine-containing organic chemicals made by industry.

Any found to be detrimental would take years to eliminate.

All of the dirty-dozen toxic persistent bioaccumulative organic chemicals, POPs, targeted for zero discharge contained chlorine.

If chlorine use was eliminated from the Great Lakes Basin, there would be no more POPs, ZERO!

It made sense to the crowd, and they went wild.

"What did the IJC commissioners do?" I asked, after Jack described the process and the emotion at the scene. "Are they going to accept this ridiculous logic? Will they forward a recommendation to ban chlorine to the EPA and Environment Canada?"

"The IJC accepted it in principle and promised to draft a recommendation," Jack said. "Then the EPA and Environment Canada will have to address banning chlorine."

"Do they know that without chlorine, we're out of business?" I asked, thinking of the devastating effect on the economy and to the health of people drinking contaminated water.

"I didn't see any dissension," Jack said. "The IJC's charter is to protect water quality."

"You'd better come back and mind the store," I said, knowing my new priority would be defense of chlorine for Great Lakes chemical-manufacturing interests.

In the quiet of my home office, I wondered if there was really anything to worry about in the third year of the popular and industry-friendly G.H.W. Bush's first term. He had appointed the three U.S. commissioners, and an equally conservative Canadian prime minister had appointed Canada's three commissioners. Would these commissioners make fools of themselves and actually recommend banning a chemical element? If they did, would the EPA and Environment Canada accept the recommendation, act upon it, and ban chlorine? Not likely, but if so . . . all

I could think of was goodbye Tin City. We would be out of business without chlorine.

The fuse to the chlorine issue had been lit. It could explode in a ban of chlorine, or smolder out as the IJC commissioners evaluated the facts and realized the ridiculousness of banning a chemical element. I couldn't imagine the IJC recommending the regional banning of a chemical element, but then gasoline without lead was once thought to be impossible, too.

It was going to be difficult to convince Upjohn's executives of the reality of this preposterous threat and the necessity to address it through political action at state and federal levels. Personally, I was feeling rather stupid. I had been in Traverse City with environmentalists, yet blindsided by IJC's environmental actions. Now, senior management was surprised by a major business threat.

My job was to prevent surprises. I didn't look forward to Monday morning.

IJC'S DECISION: MONDAY, I OCTOBER 1991

I arrived at my office early Monday morning to find my favorite picture, a Lake Superior scene, replaced by a large periodic table. The square normally occupied by chlorine was cut out and covered from behind with black matte paper.

That was the only levity for the day. A barrage of phone calls, questioning the wisdom of my consorting with the enemy and accusing me of dereliction in my duty to protect the corporate right to make chemicals, followed in rapid succession. My Tin City friends viewed an attempt to ban an element as nonsense.

I looked forward to getting out of the office to attend the Michigan Chemical Council's Government Affairs committee meeting in Lansing the next day. I would be with people who could evaluate the seriousness of the challenge to chlorine's fate. I chaired the committee and was the only member with a science or engineering background. The members were political pros, versed in the intricacies of regulation and seasoned with more than a decade of shaping rapidly developing environmental regulation for major chemical companies. They professed appreciation for my technical input, but I knew my real value was that of a fresh face from the health-care industry on the Lansing regulatory-development lobbying scene.

I held to some hope that I'd arrive to find that the pros had determined it was illegal to ban a chemical element. We'd have a laugh, wrap up the rest of our business, and go home. Frank, the committee secretary, and I had revised the agenda to include addressing the IJC's action and faxed it to all members with an urgent note to attend. I arrived early and was surprised to see a dozen people already assembled. Frank met me at the door and introduced me to the newcomers. Brad, a Washington-based lobbyist for the Chlorine Council, was surrounded by worshipful government-relations managers from major chemical companies in Ohio, New York, and Ontario. I welcomed the visitors to Michigan and proceeded to the coffee urn at the far side of the room. Frank caught my raised eyebrow and joined me.

"What's the Chlorine Council?" I asked. "Are they a big political player?"

"Weren't until this week," Frank said. "The major national chemical-manufacturing alliances are coordinating their chlorine-ban defense through them."

Nice idea, I thought. Things are going to get rough and muddy, so why get corporate or existing associations' names out front? That's how the Chlorine Council could afford someone the size of this guy receiving the rapt attention and adoration from all the industrial political pros.

"Brad's out of a Washington lobbying firm," Frank continued. "The best there is, and we've got him on loan for the duration."

I was amazed. A front organization was put together, funded, and staffed in three days. The professional lobbying infrastructure could really move when threatened. I got the answer to my biggest question: the possibility of a chlorine ban was real. My MCC agenda was reduced to one item, and the discussion shouldn't be led by an engineer.

"How about I turn the meeting over to you to introduce Brad as the chlorine discussion leader?" I said.

"You sure you want to do that?" Frank asked, having trouble holding his head from nodding as his eyes said, "Please say yes."

"Of course," I said.

"Thanks," Frank said. With his mission of "getting the amateur out of the way" accomplished, he herded the gaggle of warriors to the table.

Brad came with the blessings of all the Washington lobbying corps, a fat checkbook, and—as we soon learned—an agenda. The agenda was clear. The chemical industry would welcome study of any and all of our chemicals in a manner that was scientifically sound, and ban or restrict their use if appropriate. For the protection of public health, the use of chlorine to disinfect drinking water must remain in place. We would demonstrate that chlorine chemistry was responsible for improvements in health and well-being that were deeply woven into the fabric of the modern lifestyle. Removing chlorine would unravel that fabric.

From my engineering perspective, it seemed we were missing the point. The Great Lakes activists wanted to ban chlorine because they thought chemical-industry emissions were keeping DDT, PCBs, toxaphene, and other members of the dirty-dozen persistent organic pollutants (POPs) at unacceptable levels. Shouldn't we focus on the technical argument that we do not use, manufacture, or emit any DDT or many of the other POPs of concern? I made the mistake of asking.

"We cannot allow speculative technical possibilities onto the table to interfere with our carefully considered thrust," Brad said with a sneer that let me know this issue was in the domain of political pros, not technical amateurs.

I handle shutting up real well. I was as far out of my element as I had been at Michigan Audubon's Cause/Effect conference in Traverse City—perhaps further. Brad rolled out the strategy, identified all the players and how he was intimately connected to them, and impressed us with his support from everyone's CEO, even mine. The rest of the committee sat at the edge of their seats, in awe and rapture over his influence and power.

I tuned out and escaped to thoughts of pleasant times on Lake Superior.

While Brad impressed his cohorts with his connections and hammered home the necessity to stick to his well-defined and politically astute strategy, I continued to wonder why chlorine was going to be banned to avoid the production of chemicals already banned. Was Brad protecting another agenda? He certainly held my committee members and guests in spellbound awe.

While Brad was out of the room taking an important telephone call, I jumped at the opportunity to gain control of the meeting and push through a couple of non-chlorine agenda items. When Brad returned, he was predictably impatient, but seemed to have less starch in his Washington power shirt.

"Washington doesn't want to make this appear like a national issue," Brad said. "They'll keep the EPA out of the argument, and we'll focus political efforts at the state level. Debates at the national level will be confrontations between the Chlorine Council and activists. There will be no federal government or agency involvement until the IJC biennial."

"It appears that George Bush wants to be far away from this issue during an election year," Frank whispered after nudging me in the ribs. "Governor Engler will have to handle a major exposure while he faces reelection. We've got our work cut out."

It was accepted as a foregone conclusion that the IJC commissioners would recommend a ban. Brad regained his leadership composure and lectured the troops on the inadvisability of attempting to influence any of the president's appointed IJC commissioners, then went on to talk about the wonderful bounty of goods brought to society by chlorine. His monologue, obviously a practice for upcoming debates with activists, reminded me of my very own first product from the chlorine industry.

I was a skinny string bean, probably ten years old, shopping for a belt with my mother. The salesman showed us a plastic belt, supple as leather and as clear as water. I was hooked by this unique product of the chemical industry and convinced my mother to buy it—with room to grow, of course. In summer's heat, the belt turned soft and stretched until it went half again around me. No problem, I could easily punch a new hole through the soft material; but when I fastened the belt tight enough to hold up my pants, the holes grew into slots. My belt turned yellow, then orange. Soon it was coated with a slippery, oily substance. It would be half a century before I realized the oily material was probably PCBs, a popular plastic softener of the time.

Brad finished his monologue to broad smiles from the proud representatives of the chlorine industry. There was unanimous agreement to plan and discuss options, but not act until the IJC's recommendation was issued.

The IJC's decision[1] couldn't have been more devastating to industry if it had been written by the activists.

We know that when chlorine is used as a feedstock (chemical reactant) in the manufacturing process, one cannot necessarily predict or control which chlorinated organics will result and in what quantity. Accordingly, the commission concludes that the use of chlorine and its compounds should be avoided in the manufacturing process. We recognize that socio-economic and other consequences of banning the use of chlorine—and subsequent use of alternative chemicals or processes—must be considered in determining the timetable.

---

1. Sixth Biennial Report under the Great Lakes Water Quality Agreement of 1978 to the Governments of the United States and Canada and the State and Provincial Governments of the Great Lakes Basin.

The intent was clear: no chlorine, chlorinated reactants, chlorinated inter-mediates, or chlorinated solvents were to be used in manufacturing, and the only thing to discuss was the timing. I guess Brad's approach was right. The IJC saw a direct link between chlorine use and POPs in the Great Lakes, and trying to convince them otherwise was a waste of time.

In fewer than eighteen months, at the 1993 IJC biennial meeting, Environment Canada and the USEPA, with advice from the affected states and provinces, would decide on the IJC's chlorine-banning recommendation. The Great Lakes states and provinces would look to Michigan, the Great Lakes State, for leadership in assessing the chlorine-ban proposal. I knew the effort would require overtime, but I didn't expect the Michigan Department of Natural Resources and the Federal Fish and Wildlife Department to add to the workload by implicating my company as a POPs polluter.

THE POND: APRIL 1992

In times of frustration over the preposterous possibility of a chlorine ban, I would find peace at the edges of Upjohn's pond. In any season, it teemed with wildlife, hosting dozens of white swans, hundreds of Canada geese, and scores of wild ducks. Its waters grew trophy-sized bass and bluegill. During the spring and fall, bird watchers lined its fences to identify migrating species. In one visit, a local expert identified twenty-four different types of waterfowl. This jewel of nature at the edge of Upjohn's sprawling chemical and fermentation complex was actually a creation of Upjohn engineers.

In the early 1950s, the expansion of antibiotic fermentation facilities increased cooling-water requirements to millions of gallons per day. Cold water was pumped from the underground aquifer through the fermenter cooling coils and discharged into a nearby stream. Upjohn's engineers were concerned about the effect of warm water on the stream's trout population. They decided to send the water to a wetland area at the edge of Upjohn's property, creating an eighty-acre pond.

A ten-year period of rainfall at two-thirds the historical average dried up inland lakes and sent the Great Lakes to record low-water levels. A neighboring lake fell three feet, and Upjohn's groundwater pumping, not the deficit of rainfall, was blamed. Upjohn diverted more water to the pond, and its overflow was piped to fill up the lake. The pond cooled and percolated millions of gallons of cold water back into the aquifer for reuse, supplied needed water to a neighboring lake, and provided refuge for wildlife. In the winter of 1991, this idyllic relationship between industry, wildlife, and the community was shattered by two swans.

During cold snaps, the only ice-free water in the county, other than where our warm water flowed into the pond, was the Kalamazoo River. People in the community loved to see the geese and swans fly from their nighttime roosting on the safe and warm pond to daytime feeding areas. When two dead swans appeared on the banks of the Kalamazoo River, the Federal Fish and Wildlife Service (F&W) and Michigan's Department of Environmental Quality (DEQ) were called in to investigate. For some reason, these two normally scientific agencies assumed that the cause of the swans' fate was that they were poisoned at Upjohn's pond and died after flying to the river. There were no autopsy results and the swans had been incinerated, but we were guilty.

The DEQ was aware of our groundwater contamination and knew the pond received our discarded cooling water. They were also aware of past spills to the ground, or building roofs that had discharged to the pond. Technically, the pond on our property was "waters of the state," and our lack of a discharge permit was a serious violation. The DEQ demanded a detailed analysis of water entering our pond. The F&W informed us that killing of migratory wildfowl was a federal offense.

Water discharged to the pond contained the expected parts-per-billion amounts of chloroform and other byproducts of water chlorination, plus traces of chemicals used at the plant. Further investigation turned up parts per million of methanol. Some of our processing equipment was cooled with water, then a refrigerated methanol/water solution when lower temperatures were required. The methanol solution was recycled, but a lack of ability to completely purge equipment when switching from the methanol/water back to water cooling led to a methanol discharge to the pond. Methanol, because of its flammability and toxicity, is defined as a hazardous substance. Finding the methanol made us Michigan's largest discharger of hazardous substances to waters of the state. The DEQ was livid.

We immediately launched a study to determine the effect of these chemicals on the quality of groundwater being pumped from wells near the pond. Surprisingly, the water under the pond was pure. The pond removed pollution while cooling and recharging water. Nothing could be this good!

When informed of the outstanding treatment capability of the pond, the mood of the DEQ went from livid to ballistic. Now we were treating hazardous waste in an unlined lagoon! We were ordered to install an impermeable liner or stop sending water to the pond. The main purpose of the pond—to keep water in our local watershed by percolating it back into the ground—would be lost.

We were caught in a situation where following the law would be detrimental to the environment. With the IJC connecting the dots from industrial chlorine use to POPs, the DEQ was forced to react to the F&W allegation that POPs generated on our site were the likely cause of swan deaths. They had to be strict with us.

While the DEQ was telling us to line the pond, the F&W defined the open water body as an attractive nuisance. Migratory birds, wildlife protected by the Department of Interior's U.S. Fish and Wildlife Service, were being attracted to it and poisoned. The F&W wanted it drained—immediately—or for us to pay for every animal killed by this pot of poison.

Payment for environmental damage was a new F&W initiative. The cost of killing a fingerling trout was a hundred dollars. I imagined the price of a pair of swans would be about the cost of my house.

I was tempted to argue that these were imported mute swans and considered an invasive exotic species by serious naturalists who wanted native trumpeter swans reestablished, but knew that argument would get me nowhere. I pleaded the pond's long-term healthy web of wildlife and the unknown fate of the two incinerated swans, and offered research to assess the pond's water-treatment capability and the chemical contamination of its wildlife.

A key Michigan DEQ biologist was convinced that the pond could never be an adequate treatment system. He believed that any treatment would take place in a microscopic layer of bacteria at the pond's bottom, and if it was disturbed by nesting fish or dabbling ducks and swans, treatment capability would be disrupted until the layer was reestablished. Studies were designed and approved by the MDEQ, Michigan State University biologists, and company scientists. Tubes of soil cores were removed from the pond bottom and challenged by percolating water contaminated with various levels of chemicals through the tubes to simulate water percolating through the pond bottom. All contaminants were removed to undetectable levels, with removal taking place throughout the core, not just at the surface.

According to Michigan State University's Kellogg Biological Station researchers, methanol, the hazardous material in parts-per-million quantities, was immediately degraded by micro-life on the surface of the pond's dense vegetation. It was a welcome carbon source to the nutrient-free water, providing a vital energy supply to the bottom of the ecosystem's food chain. The university scientists said the pond ecosystem would be enhanced by an increase of methanol. The largest discharge of hazardous material to surface waters of the State of Michigan was not an ecological problem—but how about the POPs?

For half a century, the pond received discharges and spills from one of the most complex users of chlorine and chlorinated intermediates in the state. Regulators were convinced that POPs, or POPs-like compounds, would bioaccumulate up the food chain to inflict damage to ducks, geese, turtles, and swans. Proving the lack of POPs-like problems to a regulator's satisfaction would be a challenge. Proving a negative is scientifically impossible, and analyzing sediments for trace chemicals, or unaffected wildlife for possible symptoms, could chew up a healthy budget without providing definitive answers. Jim Ludwig, the independent field biologist who brought me to my POPs epiphany, provided a creative and acceptable plan.

Jim proposed using tree swallows and bioaccumulation to sample the pond. During spring breeding, tree swallows satisfy their voracious appetite for insects while feeding in a small area. If we could attract breeding pairs to the shoreline, they would consume large amounts of flying insects that had lived in larval form at the pond's bottom. Any POPs or POPs-like substance would bioconcentrate into the fat of the tree swallows, especially the yolks of their eggs. Jim engaged a colleague from Michigan State University, a specialist in the measurement of trace quantities of environmental POPs, to analyze tree-swallow egg yolks and set tree-swallow houses at the pond's edge and at two control sites.

Field data were gathered on eggs laid and chicks fledged at each site. We were relieved to find normal productivity exhibited at all sites and anxiously awaited the egg-yolk analysis. After two months, we received an unbelievable surprise.

The lack of signature chemicals from our plant site brought relief, but the shocker came from the POPs content. At all sites, the eggs contained PCBs, DDT, toxaphene, chlordane, and other banned pesticides. The scientists estimated their presence at about 25 percent of the level needed to cause eggshell thinning. The levels were virtually the same at all sites. The eggs were contaminated with banned chemicals through some manner of regional pollution, not from our operations. How were POPs getting into small, isolated inland waterways?

POPs were being found wherever they were measured, from Lake Superior to small bodies of water in our backyard. They were not coming from our chemical operations, the site of the most complex chlorine chemistry in the state, but the IJC and activists were determined to ban chlorine use to stop POPs formation. Hopefully, we could convince the state of Michigan to support continued chlorine use.

MICHIGAN'S ASSESSMENT: MAY 1992–SEPTEMBER 1993

Michigan, the "Great Lakes State," was expected to lead the effort in evaluating IJC's chlorine-ban recommendation. During his first term, Governor Engler appointed a diverse committee to prioritize the state's environmental issues. The process was scientific, open, and fair, satisfying even those who labeled the governor as anti-environmental. Governor Engler quickly announced that he would appoint a similar Science Advisory Committee to receive input and evaluate the chlorine-ban recommendation. Staffing the committee with leading academics from the state's major universities satisfied industry and the environmentalists.

Setting Governor Engler's Science Advisory Committee's objectives, guidelines, budget, logistics, and final membership lasted through his reelection in 1992—the elections that brought Bill Clinton into the presidency, with Al Gore, an avowed and dedicated environmentalist, as his vice president. For industry, this was scary. It was beyond anyone's imagination that George Bush Sr. would allow the elimination of a chemical element, but it was well within the scope of believability for the Clinton/Gore team.

Testimony to be presented to the governor's Science Advisory Committee took on a new degree of importance. I stayed with the program and supported the industry coalition in putting our defense together. In draft presentations, I tried to raise the argument that eliminating chlorine in the Great Lakes Basin would not eliminate POPs from the Great Lakes, but industry did not want to clutter their agenda with this logic.

After months of testimony, all parties were heard, and after more months of deliberation, the committee concluded that there were insufficient data to justify the banning of chlorine. Hopefully, this safe academic approach of needing more scientific proof would suffice, and the EPA and Environment Canada would not decide to ban chlorine. Recommendations from the states and provinces were advisory and did not have to be followed. If the federal agencies felt the use of chlorine presented a sufficient risk, they were obligated to err on the side of environmental protection.

While efforts to convince the governor's committee to allow chlorine use were unfolding, the collegial atmosphere was changing at the Great Lakes Regional Corporate Environmental Council (GLRCEC). This group of industrial and environmental leaders, who had been thriving and growing on discussion of Great Lakes environmental issues of mutual concern, was being torn apart by the chlorine war.

GLRCEC'S ATTEMPT: OCTOBER 1993—

The September 1991 IJC acceptance of the chlorine-ban proposal sent a shock wave through the Great Lakes Regional Corporate Environmental Council. For nearly a decade, this contingent of Great Lakes Basin industrial and environmental leadership had worked together, developed mutual trust, and learned from each other. Now, the environmentalists had blindsided the industrial community and gotten an international agency to accept a proposal that would eliminate the basin's industrial base. GLRCEC's industrial members wondered how much of the banning plans were known, or even formulated, by GLRCEC's environmental membership, who claimed the ban to be the work of a renegade coalition, not the effort of any of the mature environmental groups sitting at the Great Lakes Regional Corporate Environmental Council's table.

GLRCEC's facilitator, a Michigan Audubon Society staff member, polled the membership to solicit agenda items for the October meeting and found nobody interested in meeting. She polled the membership again, with an invitation to a November meeting to discuss the future of GLRCEC.

At the November meeting, the much cherished collegial atmosphere we had developed was enveloped in a cloud of suspicion. The atmosphere was more like our initial tentative gatherings than the congeniality and trust I had grown to savor. As the meeting progressed, little was accomplished. Every statement was being processed in the light of the chlorine ban. Mutual trust had disappeared. We were paralyzed and floundering.

By a May 1992 meeting, we decided to address chlorine. If we couldn't do it, nobody could—and if we ignored the biggest problem between us, how could we really work effectively on less important issues? We progressed, but lacked the unquestionable level of trust we had developed before the chlorine war.

At the July meeting, I was eager to learn more about cormorants I'd seen at Uncle Reino's. We had watched in awe as cormorants exited the water in front of Reino's house to fly almost straight up, and then fly single file in an undulating line that disappeared on Lake Superior's horizon. Jim Ludwig, the field researcher who kept a cross-beaked cormorant in his home swimming pool, had seen cormorants dive from the air and swim underwater, but had never seen cormorants go from swimming underwater to flying.

"We saw hundreds, maybe a thousand," I said. "Have they returned to all the Great Lakes?"

"Just the northern Great Lakes and the Finger Lakes of New York," Jim said. "Their population increase is getting worrisome to New York sportsmen."

"Why?" I asked.

"They're concentrating in areas and taking blame for removing bass and perch," Jim explained. "A group of fishermen ravaged a nesting island, shooting birds and destroying eggs."

"Will their growth be checked through harvesting?" an industrial member and avid fisherman asked.

"I cannot imagine that," an environmental member said. "Nature should be allowed to run its course."

"Is elimination of fish from the northern lakes the natural endpoint?" the fisherman asked.

"It's probably Newcastle's disease," Jim said.

"What's that?" I asked.

"Exotic Newcastle Disease—END—a virus usually entering the country through the importation of caged birds or game birds," an Audubon representative explained. "There were serious outbreaks costing hundreds of millions of dollars in 1971 and 1980. Flocks of chickens were wiped out by the disease or destroyed to keep it from spreading."

"Will it be used on the cormorants?" the fisherman asked.

"Prayed for," Jim said. "Because they congregate in close quarters, it's just a matter of time."

"If these prayers aren't answered, Audubon might respond with a little lead . . . I mean steel shot of its own," a female Audubon member said, with cheeks flushing and eyes darting.

"How could you even think of that?" a conservative environmental member countered.

"Cormorants nest in the same tree habitat the black-crowned night heron uses," the Audubon member said. "But the messy cormorant, with an appetite far exceeding his digestive capacity, despoils and kills the trees. I'd rather have night herons."

"From endangered to pest, just because the levels of PCBs and other POPs have decreased to tolerable levels," a power-company representative said. "If we can't introduce Newcastle's, can we dump the PCBs I have under secure storage? It would save me millions."

The entire group broke into hearty laughter. This was GLRCEC at its best, something I'd hoped we could regain and maintain.

Our recaptured history of dialogue, respect, and trust allowed for rapid progress in the assessing of chlorine as a GLRCEC issue. Could chlorine be used in such a way that its benefits would be realized without detriment to human health or the environment? Experts were brought in for open discussions with unlimited questioning and follow-up. Within months, we agreed on a conceptual model that would frame the issue in an unbiased manner and present a plan allowing environmental and industrial progress. Our goal was a concise document, to be helpful and informative to industry, environmentalists, and the general public. A corporate representative volunteered a neutral writer to put the concepts into an attractive draft for our review.

The draft failed GLRCEC's review. It did not openly violate the agreed-upon concepts, but they were presented in a manner that was unacceptable to the environmental leaders. Their complaint was initially unappreciated by industry members and the writer; but as we talked through concerns of the environmental membership, everyone could see that the writing, when read from an environmentalist's perspective, was biased, and we understood how the environmental leaders could not take the draft to their membership and boards for approval.

An environmental member who was associated with a university offered to try another draft. His newsletter was written by a technical-writing professor, a friend with industrial experience. Two months later, we reviewed his document with exactly the same results, but with the roles reversed.

After considerable discussion, we decided that there would be no further attempts. We had many areas of agreement, but we were incapable of writing them down in a politically safe manner. Our trust level had been developed through years of working together, but we represented industrial and environmental organizations, with membership, senior management, and boards of directors who had never experienced open dialogue with the "enemy." In the highly polarized atmosphere created by the chlorine-ban recommendation, any environmental group or industry promoting a cooperative approach would be perceived to be capitulating and selling out to the enemy.

Meetings prior to the October 1993 IJC meeting were canceled as we awaited the decision, wondering how the governments would act, and if the concept of business and environmental leaders meeting collegially could survive. The countdown had begun. All GLRCEC members would attend the IJC meeting and finish the final period of the chlorine fight as respectful individual opponents—but as an organization, GLRCEC was crippled and on the sidelines.

COUNTDOWN: NOVEMBER 1992–SEPTEMBER 1993

Chlorine-ban advocates were elated by the 1992 U.S. presidential election. Obtaining support from a second-term Republican president was difficult to imagine, but with the Clinton/Gore team in place, there was hope.

The Clinton/Gore team's early actions gave industry cause for concern. The health-care-reform campaign led by Hillary Clinton swept the country to fire up people involved in health care for proposed reforms. This was a noble cause, but she didn't include those providing hospitals, drugs, and payment in the discussions. Was this going to be the modus operandi for the next eight years of this popular new presidential couple? If so, industry could lose chlorine without a chance to present its case.

There were less visible and scarier attempts to save the environment. During their campaign, Bill Clinton and Al Gore had responded to pesticide concerns by promising a 50 percent reduction in use. Their first attempt was straightforward: a well-known pesticide commanded half the market, so eliminate it. The loss of a big-name pesticide would thrill those who worried about the traces of degradable pesticides in the environment.

However, even though extremely popular, charismatic, and politically secure, the new administration couldn't eliminate pests with their charm.

Farmers, many of whom remembered severe crop losses when DDT was eliminated and they were left defenseless against pests, were irate. Cooler heads prevailed, and the administration retreated to focus on the economy.

As the states and provinces formulated their chlorine-ban recommendations, most concluded—as Michigan had—that there was insufficient proof for such drastic action. That concerned the environmentalists, but the final decision resided with federal agencies, with their mandate to err on the side of environmental protection. Activists planned mass demonstrations to sway federal opinions, and the IJC, ever desirous of providing a forum for a "public" that would support its recommendation, accommodated their wishes.

The three American IJC commissioners were replaced with Clinton/Gore nominees. Industry was concerned about the IJC commissioners' desire and capability to control the meeting. We feared that public demonstrations and activist outrage would be the only input into the EPA and Environment Canada's decision on our future.

Industry had to be at the IJC meeting and prepared, this time. We could not afford to be blindsided again. The Chlorine Council hired Paul, a charismatic retired automotive executive, to develop and lead industry's presentation. Getting time on IJC's agenda provided him with his first challenge. Industry would have to present its defense of chlorine in a twenty-minute slot following a children's demonstration.

While the days wound down, we polished our presentation and anxiously awaited the EPA's decision. Would they really accept a proposal to ban chlorine? Would they tip their hand before the meeting? Shortly before the meeting, Environment Canada made the first move, stating they could not, on the available data, accept the decision to ban chlorine at this time. The USEPA and Environment Canada frequently traded barbs concerning who was the superior environmental protector, and we worried about the possibility of the EPA upstaging Environment Canada. With a sigh of relief, we heard EPA support Environment Canada's decision on the day before the meeting.

The environmentalists took the perceived lack of data as a challenge to provide the EPA and Environment Canada with overwhelming evidence. If the EPA and Environment Canada wanted more data, they should come to Windsor and get it!

THE IJC MEETING: THURSDAY, 22 OCTOBER 1993, WINDSOR, ONTARIO

The IJC meeting was kicked off with a debate between Brad and an environmental leader. The attendants in business suits and shiny shoes appeared ill at ease among the activists, a long-haired majority in denim, flannel, and muslin with sneakers or hiking boots. The activists looked intense and expectant, eager to win back the governments' support. TV cameras were in place, and a dozen reporters were finishing pre-debate questioning of speakers and government officials.

Brad, in a dark blue pin-striped suit accented by a broad-striped red and white tie, began the debate. His firm features gave him a commanding appearance, and his face appeared much kinder on stage than in meeting rooms. The captain is going to take us on a ride in his jumbo jet, I thought. The audience was taken on a twenty-minute cruise of the wonders of chlorine. Brad was rewarded with polite applause from the suits as the activists buzzed in disbelief.

An articulate young anti-chlorine researcher from Oregon represented the Coalition of International Environmental Organizations. In his flannel shirt with rolled-up sleeves, blue jeans, and hiking boots, he approached the podium and hesitated a moment . . . like a TV evangelist. He ran his fingers through wavy rust-colored locks, flashed a charming smile, and took the audience on a fast-paced tour through the chlorine graveyard, concluding that there was no reason to allow the industry to continue to exist, much less continue to grow. A thunderous outburst of standing applause and shouts of "Zero Now" and "No More Chlorine" erupted, and dozens of activists snake-danced placards around the hall.

The speakers and the audience reaction had not consumed the allotted time, so the moderator called a break to set up for the next presentations. The only questioning was done by the TV crew as they interviewed the environmental leader lingering on stage, carefully positioning the cameraman to catch the demonstrating activists in the background. The industry group followed Brad's lead and exited the room.

I was disappointed; I had really expected something more than the same old spiels from both sides. I left the room for a stretch.

"Care to join us for a debriefing?" Frank, from the Michigan Chemical Council, asked as he passed.

"No thanks. I'm going to take in the technical sessions," I said.

"Stop by after and let us know how they went," Frank replied over his shoulder.

The auditorium was less than half full for a paper industry's presentation on dioxin-elimination progress, to be followed by a panel discussion of POPs-induced endocrine disruption. The paper-company engineer's first slide was a pie chart showing paper-pulp bleaching as North America's major source of dioxin. When the slide hit the screen, cries of "polluter," "industry hack," and "killer" rose from the audience. The speaker stood in his baggy gray flannel pants and blue blazer, fumbling with his red tie and adjusting pens in the pocket protector of his blue cotton shirt. He killed the slide and the crowd quieted.

His next slide, entitled "The Chemistry of Chlorine Dioxide," brought the house to their feet again, shouting "No more chlorine!" The engineer looked to the moderator for help, but the moderator turned away. The assembled panel of environmental toxicologists waiting their turn to discuss endocrine disruption tittered and shared smiles. The engineer continued his slides at a flash-card pace, allowing no time for audience interaction.

My grasp of the rapid-fire presentation was that chlorine dioxide, a compound of chlorine and oxygen, was a very effective bleaching agent. There was no dioxin detected in the effluent of a mill converted to chlorine dioxide at significant capital and operating expense. The speaker emphasized his industry's willingness to bear the cost. He sighed in relief when the final slide passed and the room darkened. The moderator raised the lights, called for questions, and recognized a man identifying himself as the research director for Greenpeace.

"Sir," he asked the engineer, "you said that there was no dioxin in the discharge from the test plant. Is that correct?"

"Yes," the engineer replied with a smile of satisfaction at the easy and helpful question. "It's undetectable."

"I also understand that chlorine dioxide dissociates in water to form chlorine," the researcher probed. "Is that correct?"

"To a minor extent," the engineer said.

"Then you do agree that chlorine will be present in water containing chlorine dioxide?"

The engineer cringed, not wanting to answer. "Theoretically," he finally replied.

"Then, since the same conditions are present in chlorine bleaching, isn't it reasonable that this chemical soup would produce dioxin?"

"It's undetectable," the engineer said.

"The fact that your analytical lab can't measure it doesn't mean there's none there. Can you assure us that there isn't a single molecule of dioxin there?"

The engineer shifted his weight from one leg to the other. "No, but—"

"No buts about it," the questioner shouted. "You people still don't get it. Zero means zero!"

The crowd was livid. A dozen activists paraded around the room, shouting, "No more chlorine. Zero now. Zero! Zero! Zero!"

The engineer hastily gathered his materials and fled the room.

During the endocrine-disruption panel discussion, each of four researchers gave a short presentation and then questioned each other. The scientific details were esoteric and elusive, but the basic concepts were within my grasp. Their research implicated POPs in serious health problems other than cancer. Theo Colburn was one of the panelists. Suddenly I remembered her presentation with Jim Ludwig at the Traverse City, Michigan, meeting two years previous. "The Human Cancer Paradigm Reviewed: An Inadequate Means to Protect Piscivorous Great Lakes Wildlife and Humans" had been embraced by this group of scientists, who credited very low concentrations of POPs with causing wildlife and human problems. Pollutants at a thousandth of the cancer-causing level could mimic endocrines, the natural chemical messengers that controlled processes in living cells. This disruptive process was proven to cause birth defects in laboratory animals.

The researchers drew a link between POPs in the environment and human diseases ranging from sperm-count decline to birth defects, increased prison populations, and learning disabilities. Significant research needs were identified because only a fraction of the specific congeners and impurities of PCBs and other POPs had been studied for cancer, and their endocrine-disruption capability was virtually unknown. Some POPs showed increasing negative effects with decreasing concentration. Anything other than zero was intolerable.

The activists erupted in applause and shouts of "Zero now!" giving the presentation a standing ovation rare in academic circles. The researchers, glowing in the appreciation of the cheering crowd, congratulated themselves at the podium. The moderator thanked the presenters individually and as a group before inviting the crowd to the next day's sessions.

I went to the industry suite to report on the meetings and to check in with Paul. He needed to register a complaint about the shabby treatment given the paper-company engineer.

The room was full of milling executives and public-relations pros. Most of them were gathered around Brad, congratulating him on the fine debate. Frank waved me over.

"Paul has some great news," Frank said, directing me toward the retired automotive executive in charge of our presentation. "Tell him, Paul."

"We've garnered the Chemical Workers Union support," Paul said. "They lost a lot of jobs when CFCs were banned to protect the ozone layer, and they don't want to be decimated by a chlorine ban."

"Congratulations," I said. "That's a real boost."

"It'll require tweaking our presentation," Frank said.

"Just a little," Paul said. "Could you cut from four to three minutes to give them some time?"

"After seeing what the crowd of activists did to the paper-company's presentation, I'll give you my four minutes," I said with a laugh that must have sounded like I was less than half joking.

"I can't accept that," Paul said. "We need your presentation."

"How bad was it?" Frank asked.

"Totally out of control," I said, "and the moderators didn't lift a finger to help. The activists drowned out the presentation of any visuals. He had to kill the slides to quiet them, and then run through at a speed that was too fast for them to react."

"Or for anybody to understand," Frank said.

"There's nothing controversial on tomorrow's agenda," I said. "Then Saturday starts with the governments' presentations. I wonder if they'll get any respect."

"I'll speak to the commissioners," Paul said. "We should be assured of some semblance of civility."

Brad caught the last of our conversation. "Don't be scared off by a little noise and a few catcalls," he said. "We'll prevail, but we've got to stick with our agenda. We can count on you, can't we?"

"Certainly," I said, more to assure myself than Brad.

I always liked public speaking, but I'd never faced an audience whose total focus was disruption. Good thing I had a day to trim and practice my talk.

I planned to stay out of the political arena for a day and take in some relaxing scientific sessions.

IJC SCIENCE: FRIDAY, 23 OCTOBER 1993, WINDSOR, ONTARIO

If the opening-night agenda was crafted to create media-attracting controversy and arouse environmental activists, it worked. On my way to the technical sessions, two hotel meeting rooms were full of coeds feverishly sorting and repairing white robes and lining boxes with black cloth. In the parking lot, a group of young men were constructing boxes from scrap lumber.

The chlorine-dioxide talk of the past night was intriguing; I wanted to learn more. I wondered if it was "smoke and mirrors" technology, or a real breakthrough. It sounded too good to be true. I went to the exhibition floor, found the chlorine-dioxide manufacturer's display, and recognized the person manning the booth: the son of a friend from work.

"Good to see you, Walt," I said. "Thought you were selling computers."

"Got into this a year ago," Walt said. "Best environmental technology I've ever seen."

I expressed my lack of familiarity and desire to know more.

"There's a technical presentation on a British Columbian installation starting in five minutes," Walt said. "The presenters were key people in the design and implementation of the project."

I hoped the presenters would get a chance to speak this time; I really wanted to know if the technology worked. Dioxin, one of the most toxic substances known to man, was the first of the POPs identified in the Great Lakes, and in some regions the biggest contributor to total POPs toxicity. As conditions required for its formation and destruction became understood, its anthropogenic (man-made) generation rate fell dramatically. It was still present in the Great Lakes, but its contribution to the total POPs toxicity had been eclipsed by PCBs and DDT.

Bleaching of paper pulp, the largest recognized generator of dioxin, was under intense scrutiny from activists and regulators. Most Great Lakes Basin chlorine-bleaching facilities had shut down, forcing bleaching operations nearer to logging sites. The presentation would describe the experience of a large paper-pulp manufacturer in an isolated British Columbian valley. Trout in the river receiving the mill's effluent had high dioxin levels and couldn't reproduce.

The company was implicated and its guilt obvious. They offered to switch from chlorine to chlorine dioxide in the bleaching process and were willing to incur increased costs to stay in business. Canadian regulators and environmentalists made them monitor the environment to assure that their promised results were realized in the field.

I arrived at the meeting while the speakers were being introduced. The room was small and the crowd sparse. The first speaker described the field-monitoring project. Before making any changes, they performed a baseline study on trout dioxin levels and continued to follow contamination and health throughout the project. The baseline study showed mildly contaminated trout upstream from the plant, and highly contaminated non-reproducing trout downstream.

The second speaker admitted that the plant's effluent contained significant dioxin before the start of the project. The first stage of the project eliminated part of the chlorine, and improvement in the effluent was noted. Months later, when all the necessary equipment was installed, chlorine use ceased. With 100 percent chlorine-dioxide use, quality paper was produced and there was no dioxin measured in the effluent.

The first speaker correlated his field data with the project. The dioxin levels in the trout decreased with time, and after the total conversion to chlorine dioxide, the dioxin levels in the trout tailed off to become equivalent to the upstream trout. He estimated the half-life of dioxin in trout (the time for the concentration to reduce 50 percent) to be six months.

This was fantastic news! Chlorine dioxide really worked, and when not exposed to dioxin, contaminated trout metabolized or somehow eliminated dioxin. Too bad only fifty people, and no reporters, heard it.

What about the dioxin in the upstream trout? How are they getting contaminated? I was just about to raise my hand when the speaker explained.

They were concerned about the background contamination and sampled trout from a nearby valley, finding the same background contamination. They removed a sediment core from an impoundment supplied by the river and sampled increments to correlate dioxin deposition with time. Historical samples, from depths representing pre-industrial times, had a low-level background of dioxin, with minor variations. At the depth equivalent to the date of the bleaching-plant start-up, the dioxin levels rose dramatically.

Their conclusion was that the area had a natural source of dioxin, probably forest fires. There would be no zero! Where were last night's noisy activists?

The media? Only a few people—a smattering of municipal, academic, and industrial representatives—heard this fantastic story.

The opening session of the "State of the Health of Lake Superior" had an entirely different flavor. The head of a national environmental organization kicked off the session with an inspiring description of the pristine beauty and diversity of healthy wildlife once supported by our largest and uppermost Great Lake, a lake that due to its remote location and lack of intensive human intrusion might still be salvaged from chlorine's talons. He urged the room, this time packed with activists, to spare no energy in saving this jewel from a chlorinated fate. He ended his plea with the rallying cry of "If not here, where?" "If not us, who?" and "If not now, when?" to enthusiastic cheers and the constant attention of a TV cameraman.

The speaker reminded us that the Lake Superior watershed had been proposed as a "demonstration area" at the 1991 IJC meeting, and since then, environmental activists had been successful in killing a proposed pulp mill in Michigan's Lake Superior watershed.

The next speaker, an ecological-planning specialist, presented a detailed plan to move all people away from the lakeshore, ban chlorine, and shut down all mines, mills, ports, and factories. According to him, subsidizing people in their efforts to survive on ecotourism and nonpolluting cottage industries would be a small price for the protection of this salvageable resource.

The cadre of Lake Superior basin's municipal utility managers, who'd come to Windsor to see if the IJC was really serious, were irate. They stood as a unit to question the sanity of the proposal, and were shouted down as they pled for chlorine to protect their drinking-water systems and control coliform in waste-treatment effluents. Was the Canadian port city of Thunder Bay, Ontario, supposed to stop loading Canadian grain into freighters bound for the global market and disappear into the woods? Would Marquette, Michigan, and Duluth, Minnesota, be obliterated, and the shipment of iron ore, coal, and road salt be made by road and rail? Would the mines and mills throughout northern Michigan, Wisconsin, and Minnesota be abandoned?

The speaker, along with the organization's national leader, left without answering questions, followed by activists and the cameraman. A small, quiet, and somber group stayed for the technical sessions.

A survey of dioxin sources determined that most of the dioxin entering Lake Superior came from local open burning of trash. A sophisticated analytical study indicated that more than 80 percent of the PCBs entering Lake Superior came from the air. Because there was little industry or population in the Lake Superior basin, I began to wonder how far the air carried the PCBs. The theme of the 1993 IJC meeting, "Think Basin-Wide," was picked to encourage participants to expand their thinking. Was basin-wide expanded far enough?

I left the meetings amazed at the findings. First, dioxin was ever-present in the Canadian north woods; second, dioxin from the major anthropogenic source could be controlled; and third, most of the PCBs in Lake Superior got there through the air. With a twinge of fear about contaminants in fish, I picked up a greasy sausage in a bun at the park and relaxed in the autumn sunshine. A group of activists congregated around a guitar player and sang protest songs as office workers jogged past. A band of Walpole Ojibwas prepared signs and banners to demonstrate against the Ontario government for allowing a chemical company to pollute their water. Other activists raised and immediately lowered a large banner near the street directly across from Cleary Convention Centre.

The banner was paraded quickly around the park and packed into a waiting van. "Dow Shalt Not Kill," read the black block letters, dripping in blood red. Dow, a major manufacturer of chlorine and chlorinated chemicals, was headquartered in Midland, Michigan, and had garnered infamy among activists for manufacturing the defoliant Agent Orange. Dioxin, an impurity in Agent Orange, was implicated in numerous diseases and disorders stemming from the Vietnam War. We'll probably see that sign again, I thought.

THE SHOWDOWN: SATURDAY, 24 OCTOBER 1993, WINDSOR, ONTARIO

On the way out of my hotel, I held the door for a coed with an armload of costumes. "Don't miss the presentations today," she said. "We're ready for them."

They certainly looked ready for something: a dozen people were loading two vans and several cars. In the quiet and empty park, city maintenance crews were cleaning up the bottles, cans, and rubbish of the past night's revelry.

By the time I returned from breakfast and a walk around town, I was surprised by the number of people milling about the park and the display of signs and banners with anti-chlorine slogans. Absentmindedly, I got stuck in the midst of a band of picketing Walpole Ojibwas crossing the street to the Cleary Centre. I saw TV cameras and suppressed a grin when I thought of the folks back home watching the evening news and seeing my smiling face sticking out of a band of grim-faced picketers.

I slipped into the back of the main auditorium, catching the last words introducing an EPA deputy director. The outside glass wall, behind the podium, overlooked the park. When the EPA executive took the microphone, the large banner "DOW SHALT NOT KILL; BAN CHLORINE, raised outside, and was greeted by applause and exuberant cheering inside. The speaker shuffled his notes and looked around, pleasantly surprised by the unexpected welcome. He looked out the window and returned to reality to tell the audience about the EPA's tremendous progress with the Toxics Reduction Inventory, or TRI—the program requiring industries to disclose their release of scores of chemicals to air, water, or land. Companies, seeing their emissions reported in local newspapers, reacted voluntarily, making reductions of millions of pounds of toxic releases at a record pace. The EPA promised expanded regulations to include more chemicals, smaller amounts of acceptable levels, and inclusion of more industries until zero discharge was a reality. Nothing was said about banning chlorine.

I began to understand the governments' focus on Pollution Prevention. The Toxics Reduction Inventory had spawned reductions in solvent emissions, and they were hoping to keep it going through an extensive Pollution Prevention program. Even though I couldn't see a connection between toxics reduction and POPs in the environment, perhaps the EPA executive thought the activists would. The activists came to act, not to listen.

While he was speaking, a group paraded a billboard-sized "Citizen's Report Card" around the hall. It graded the agency on various activities, and the grades were not good. The activist public was dissatisfied with their government, and the IJC meeting provided an outlet for their outrage.

"What a circus," Frank said, sitting down beside me. "Glad they're venting on the government instead of us."

The end of the deputy director's report touched off a parade of placards and people costumed as birds and animals. A club-footed bald eagle, a fish with huge tumors, and a cross-beaked cormorant showed the horrors wrought by continuing use of chlorine.

When Environment Canada's administrator took the podium, the cross-beaked cormorant paced in front of the hall, faced the speaker, and hissed at his points. The flustered speaker lost his place and stumbled badly. The cormorant waved goodbye, to the speaker's relief and the crowd's delight.

On my way to the final planning session for the industry presentation, I stopped at a university booth.

"I've heard about transport modeling," I said to the graduate student. "How does it work?"

"Sensitive detection equipment is placed on a tower to continuously monitor contaminants," she said. "Contaminant data are computer-integrated with a powerful weather model. When a spike in concentration occurs, the computer can backtrack to the contaminant source."

"Have you done this?" I asked.

"The technology is in its infancy," she said. "Detailed weather data, complex models, and larger computers are needed. It will be a couple of years."

I meandered through the displays and joined Frank at the industry room. An executive, returning from watching activists harass the government speakers, had just entered the room.

"Are we going to honor this circus by participating in it?" he thundered, and not hearing an immediate response, added, "Their treatment has been nothing short of rude. There's no crowd control. We won't be listened to. Let's pack it in."

The attendees looked around at the dissenting executive, toward Paul (the presentation leader), and at each other. There was sympathy for the man's opinion, especially among those of us with speakers' nametags.

Paul seized the conversation. "If we fold now, we'll be playing right into their hands," he said, beginning to pace like a coach whose team needed uplifting. "We've got a great story to tell, one that all of us can be proud of. We're the major contributor to improved lifestyle and life span. We're willing to subject all of our chemicals to a science-based process of evaluation that would lead to their banning if proven dangerous. We have nothing to be ashamed of."

Paul stopped in front of the dissenter, placing a hand on his shoulder. "What about it?" he asked.

"You're right," the dissenter replied, shaking his head.

The afternoon session began with activist presentations, which were applauded and paraded. Late in their agenda, the audience was treated to entertainment from a group of schoolchildren from Windsor and Detroit. They danced onto the stage like freshly hatched butterflies, angelic in the white robes I'd seen being made at the hotel. To the meeting-weary participants representing environmentalists, industry, and government—especially those who were fathers and mothers—they were a welcome relief.

Before their songs ended, two coeds costumed as grim reapers carried a large black casket labeled "The Not So Great Lakes" onto the stage. Individual children stepped forward with items to place in the casket. A parade of boxes labeled terns, gulls, eagles, trout, mink, cormorant, and otter were somberly laid to rest as the angelic choir exited and a young girl gave a speech of concern. They loved the wildlife of the Great Lakes and hoped that the people present would take necessary actions to guarantee that they and their children would have birds, fish, and animals to enjoy in the future.

The industry presentation was next. "A hard act to follow," Paul mumbled, and took the podium to introduce me.

"We've lost a little time," an IJC commissioner said before Paul got to the microphone. "Would you be so kind as to be brief?"

"Certainly," Paul said, looking at his watch. "We'll do our planned agenda, let you hear from the labor representatives we've added, and make up your time." He went into succinct summary of what they'd learn from our presentation and introduced me.

The crowd was restless and buzzing but not unruly during Paul's introduction. Maybe this wouldn't be another circus—or maybe they were tired, or interested in seeing our bond with labor.

"Take your time," Paul said with a twinkle in his eye as we passed.

I placed my notes on the podium and looked up, panning the crowd. I shouldn't have. The "Dow Shalt Not Kill" banner was moved inside and faced me from the left-rear corner of the large room. To the right, a band of people were holding bed sheets covered with writing. I recognized Mary, an activist from Kalamazoo, holding the front edge of the leading sheet. I realized I wasn't here for the view and looked down at my notes to start my talk. Out of the corner of my left eye, I saw something move. I started talking and kept looking down as I felt the presence of something in front of me.

I made a convincing point and looked up . . . directly into the eyes of the hissing cross-beaked cormorant. I was transfixed and lost focus as I tried to see beyond the costume and talk to myself about maintaining control. I looked down and continued talking.

When the next major point was made, I looked over the disturbing beast . . . right into a dozen people who stood and waved placards on sticks. "Greed,"

"Liar," and "Industry Hack" were some of their messages. I wasn't there to read messages. I looked down at my notes and continued talking.

The next time I made a good point, I looked over the placards to the back of the room, thinking I could look past the offending messages . . . wrong. Mary was standing to the left of her unfurled bed sheet. It was a statement of our Toxic Release Inventory, along with one-liners covering every environmental sin she thought we'd committed. Mary shouted my name along with a defaming accusation.

I'm not here to read bed sheets, I told myself. There was no way I'd finish a talk with my head down, but I had nowhere to look. My knees shook and my brow glistened with sweat. I gripped the podium for support, wondering how much fear my face projected. I could hear that I was still talking, but had no idea what I was saying.

I suddenly remembered the offer of help from Elaine, a Dow public-relations specialist helping us with our presentation. "If it gets rough," she said, "I'll be sitting four rows back and to your right. I'll be a friendly face in the crowd if you need one." I looked up, even though I wasn't completing a major point. The cormorant hissed and flapped his wings. I looked to the right. Elaine was wearing a red, white, and blue sweater. She should stand out in this crowd. Where was she? I thought I'd spotted her just as I had to return to my notes.

The next time I looked up, I looked directly into the warmest, friendliest, sweetest brown eyes I'd ever seen. Elaine was smiling and flashing me a "two thumbs up" with her hands against her sweater. The talk got easier, and the rivers of sweat slowed to trickles. The cormorant caught on and moved to my right, but by then I'd settled into a groove and finished without incident. Boos and catcalls drowned out the polite industrial applause.

As I returned to my seat, Mary and her partner paraded their bed sheet in front of the smiling commissioners, then in front of the audience.

"Good job, partner," Paul whispered as he returned from introducing the next speaker. "Who's the friend calling you by name?"

"One of our finest county commissioners," I said.

"They don't pay you enough," Paul said.

During Paul's wrap-up of the industry talks, a chain of bed-sheet banners and frenzied humans ringed the entire auditorium. Every major company in the basin was represented on a sheet displaying the company's Toxic Release Inventory emission numbers, and choice, slanderous words.

The labor representatives expressed concern about the loss of jobs should the IJC be successful in banning chlorine. CFCs had been banned to protect the ozone layer, and hundreds of jobs were lost. They had good, high-paying jobs and didn't want to end up "flipping burgers."

The IJC commissioners assured them of adequate compensation if they were to lose their jobs to a successful chlorine ban.

"You did well!' Frank said at our wrap-up.

"Couldn't have made it without Elaine," I said, giving her a hug. "Thanks."

"Took you a long time to find me," Elaine said, smiling. "Were you distracted?"

"See you at our meeting next week," Frank said. "Have a safe trip home."

On the ride home, something about the meeting bothered me. Other than the unruly circus atmosphere the IJC promoted for the activists, it had really been interesting and educational, but the whole chlorine fight still felt like a misguided effort. Previously, environmental scientists had sought and obtained rigorous cause/effect relationships when proving that chemicals killed or prevented reproduction of wildlife. The chlorine-ban recommendation was accepted without the scientific rigor of a cause/effect analysis. Neither IJC scientists nor the industrial community gave serious thought to the cause/effect relationship between the use of chlorine in the basin and the presence of POPs in the Great Lakes. The IJC scientists tittered with delight as they watched industry being shouted down by activists, and business leaders refused to address any argument other than the overwhelmingly positive attributes of chlorine-containing chemicals and the offer to test and ban any of them. The banning of chlorine was probably behind us, but there was no closure on the cause of lingering contamination of the Great Lakes.

The governments had done all they could to eliminate POPs; they'd banned them. Now the USEPA and Environment Canada projected overly optimistic rates of reduction in future contamination levels and pinned their hopes on Pollution Prevention, an effort lacking a cause/effect relationship to POPs. Lake Superior was still in trouble!

The science sessions were informative, but would any of the research efforts determine why Lake Superior was not getting cleaner? Would the modeling studies find continuing POPs sources? Were they coming from the basin or beyond? I didn't know, but knew I wouldn't be content until I could understand how 80 percent of Lake Superior's PCBs arrived through the air—and if other POPs arrived by the same route. When POPs got to Lake Superior, was it the end of the road, or could they leave Lake Superior? I suddenly entered the environment of a mystery novel—a mystery with chemicals as characters.

Because the behavior of POPs in the environment was not well understood, industry and activists had widely differing opinions of POPs fate. Industry assumed that POPs quickly degraded, or were buried in sediments. Environmentalists assumed that the Great Lakes were a magnet for POPs, attracting and retaining them forever. Careful observation and research would be needed to find the truth lying somewhere between these polarized assumptions. Or would the truth lie outside the current arguments? It was time to stop defending chlorine use and start searching for answers.

THE SEARCH: 1994–2000

SOLEC: OCTOBER 1993–OCTOBER 1994

My up-close and personal experience with the cross-beaked cormorant and hecklers in Windsor left me feeling like I was the worst-treated person, and industry the most humiliated group, at the IJC meeting. With a little thought and empathy, I could have realized how insulting the process was to the USEPA and Environment Canada. Industry did not have to be there; we fought for a spot on the agenda. Not so for the governmental agencies.

The 1978 revisions to the United States and Canada's water-quality agreement required the two countries to "restore and maintain the chemical, physical, and biological integrity of the waters of the Great Lakes Basin Ecosystem." As part of that agreement, the respective environmental agencies were required to report regularly on progress toward several general and specific objectives. The IJC received those reports and gave the environmental-activist community the opportunity to judge their governments' performance in a manner that provided a platform for pickets in 1989, a chlorine ban in 1991, and a circus in 1993.

The governments disliked reporting to a forum featuring speculative science and attracting a public interested in expressing outrage. Environment Canada and the USEPA thought of themselves as science-based, had scientifically defined objectives, and sought to interact with the public in a calm and considered atmosphere.

"The EPA, through an academic intermediary, asked for our opinion and support for a science-based biennial forum," Frank said at November's Michigan Manufacturers Council meeting. "They and Environment Canada have concluded that IJC's mandate to receive reports at biennial meetings is an assumed and presumptuous role."

"The report is required," Jerry (Frank's young lawyer understudy) said. "But not to the IJC."

"Will they just write and publish the report?" I asked, thinking they'd take that path to avoid the cormorant, signs, and catcalls.

"They desire public input and are proposing a scientific forum," Jerry said. "Their working title is 'State of the Lakes Ecosystem Conference,' or SOLEC."

"How will they keep out the animals and bed sheets?" I asked.

"Only those actively involved in research, or holding a leadership position in the basin's regulatory, industrial, municipal, academic, or serious NGO (non-governmental organization) advocate organizations will be allowed to register," Jerry said.

"There will be no effort to discriminate against anyone except the disruptive element the IJC has promoted," Frank said.

"What do they want from us?" I asked.

"The EPA is anticipating uproar from the Clinton-appointed IJC commissioners," Frank said. "They would like passive support for SOLEC's concept, and some quiet lobbying to let key folks in the Clinton administration and Congress know that a scientific forum is good for all parties."

"We are in support of this," Jerry said, looking around. "Aren't we?"

"Think about it," Frank said. "The only research getting attention is toxics. Ecosystem research is suffering from the focus on chemicals."

That's all the assembled chemical manufacturers needed to hear: an opportunity to take the heat off chemicals. Sure, they supported the idea, and everyone had a contact in a key place to convince them of SOLEC's superior approach. The first meeting of the State of the Lakes Ecosystem Conference was held in Detroit in October 1994.

Activists were livid about being locked out of a meeting on their lakes' environment. A national environmental leader used his co-contribution to the keynote address to call the Great Lakes industries "wolves in sheep's clothing," as they preached environmentalism while increasing their use of chlorine. He was not among the environmental leaders staying to network and communicate.

The agenda focused on research needs to measure trends in the ecosystem through scientific and reliable indicators. I was amazed at what wasn't known about the Great Lakes' food chain and the magnitude of nonchemical threats facing the lakes.

A serious and understandable threat was loss and degradation of shoreline habitat. In my travels, I'd seen the shoreline building up with marinas, condominiums, and mansions. The aquatic scientists were concerned that a focus of research money on POPs, and federal funding to dredge contaminated sediments, would lead to Great Lakes without chemical contamination . . . and without fish-producing habitats. The first wave of environmental action took an ecosystem that couldn't produce fish because of oxygen depletion and made a system full of contaminated fish. The current path could lead to an even more dramatic effect . . . no fish.

SOLEC was proving to be informative and sensible, until I ventured into a talk on Pollution Prevention by a Washington think tank. Their inch-thick report concluded that reduction in the millions of pounds of toxic emissions to the Great Lakes Basin's air and water would remove the POPs. G. Tracy Mehan, director of Michigan's Great Lakes Protection Fund, had funded the study and was holding a stack of reports as if they were his first grandchildren. I had talked with Tracy before, knew him as a straight shooter, and could not allow him to continue believing in a connection between "toxics" emissions and POPs.

"Good to see you, Mel," he said, offering his free hand. "Want a copy?"

"As a joke sheet," I said, taking one. "I'll send it back to you in twenty years so you can laugh too."

"What are you driving at?" he asked, and then waved me off when I opened my mouth. "Give it to me in terms a lawyer with a history major can understand."

"It's simple," I said, shrugging my shoulders. "There's no way to make POPs out of toxics emissions. There is not a chemical path between solvents, paint thinners, alcohols, other low-molecular-weight emissions, and POPS."

"No way?"

"None."

"It's a perfect fit with historical data," Tracy countered.

"Only if the right time frame is picked," I said.

"You sure there's no way?"

"There's not a path from A to B."

"Sure?"

"Positive."

Director Mehan stepped back, cupped his chin in his free hand, and studied me for a moment. He then surprised me with an unbelievable invitation.

"There's an industrial opening coming up on Michigan's Great Lakes Protection Fund's Scientific Advisory Board," he said. "I'd love to have you if you're interested."

I was dumbfounded. Generally, people seek a diversity of individuals who agree with them for board members, not a critic. What a refreshing attitude! "I'd love to," I said." Send me the details."

At the conclusion of SOLEC 1994, a panel of speakers assembled for brief wrap-up statements, followed by a question-and-answer session led by a Chicago radio personality. The national environmental keynote speaker returned to bemoan the fate of Lake Superior and the desire to save it from a toxic fate at any cost. He wanted action, starting with moving people and industry away from its shores.

I was bothered. If Lake Superior was really getting 80–90 percent of its PCBs from the air, what good would abandoning the shores do? I must be missing something, I thought, and asked, "If all people and industry were moved out of the Lake Superior Basin and 90 percent of the PCBs entering the lake are coming from the air, how long would it be before the trout knew the people were gone?"

The panel squirmed. A few were sympathetic to the idea of retreating from Lake Superior to save it, but hadn't really thought about how people affected the Lake Superior ecosystem compared to the effect of its surrounding air.

"Good question," a relieved municipal representative from Thunder Bay, Ontario (Canada's largest Lake Superior community) shouted from the audience.

"Let's have a good answer," his cohort from Marquette, Michigan, added.

The panelists looked at each other. Finally the environmental leader spoke: "These chemicals are so terrible that we should do all we can to eliminate all that can be eliminated until we achieve zero."

That was not an answer, but it got the session to its next question. At the end of the session, I spotted a woman making her way through the crowd with a stack of pamphlets in her hand.

"Thought you might appreciate this," she said, handing me a magazine-sized paper entitled "Mystery on the Great Lakes." It was a well-illustrated explanation of the transport of POPs over long distances.

Her Environment Canada atmospheric-research station near Toronto, Ontario, measured POPs in the air and noticed a different spectrum of POPs in samples taken on different days. Integrating the results with meteorological data showed air arriving at Toronto from Mexico and the western United States to be different from air coming up from the Gulf of Mexico. I thumbed through the report, thanked her for it, and she left without inviting further discussion.

After I got a chance to study the report, I wondered why this new and interesting finding did not get a spot on the SOLEC agenda. SOLEC supported an aggressive air-monitoring program. There were rather limited data, and the report did point out that Canada still used a POPs pesticide banned in the United States, but why not subject these early findings to scientific scrutiny? It was a very interesting modeling study, and I hoped there would be more studies of how POPs traveled in air.

Meanwhile, the USEPA, along with the IJC, was interested in a new concept, that of a Great Lakes airshed. I hoped to hear more.

AIRSHED: 1994–1995

With SOLEC's emphasis on habitat loss, scientific understanding of the food chain, and the continuing invasion of exotic species, scientists concerned about POPs feared the end of chemical-contamination concerns. I was certainly sympathetic to that viewpoint. The Great Lakes were on the edge of their ability to support wildlife, and any introduction of a new POP, or increase of an existing threat could be disastrous. The continuing sources of POPs, or the mechanism that kept them in the Great Lakes, had to be found.

Annual reports of POPs levels in the Great Lakes were closely followed and the newly issued data eagerly anticipated. In Lake Michigan, the PCB and DDT concentrations continued a slow downward trend. Lake Superior PCB concentrations stayed constant, and toxaphene was showing up wherever samples were measured in the northernmost Great Lakes. In the cold, clear northern waters, toxaphene was present at twice the PCB concentration. A concerted scientific effort to find their source was needed; maybe GLRCEC could revitalize and tackle the challenge.

Unfortunately, memories of the chlorine-ban battle had left a dialogue-smothering cloud over the Great Lakes Regional Corporate Environmental Council (GLRCEC). Industrial members saw the defeat of the chlorine ban as a victory for their position of willingness to subject all their chemicals to scientific scrutiny and ban them if necessary. Environmentalists clung to the belief that errant chlorine chemistry within the basin was sustaining the

Great Lakes POPs levels. As individuals, the members of GLRCEC didn't wish to disband, but obtaining financial support and time for meeting attendance was becoming difficult after the polarizing effects of the IJC meetings. Attendance dropped, and the hopeful remnant attempted to prioritize Great Lakes environmental issues and again find one we could address.

Environmental members brought forth a glimmer of hope when the USEPA approached them concerning their "airshed" approach, a way to achieve POPs reduction without banning chlorine. Perhaps this issue would allow us to recapture our collegial spirit. Although regulators, lawmakers, and media were excluded from GLRCEC membership and attendance, we agreed to invite an EPA representative to explain the concept of a Great Lakes airshed.

The Great Lakes Basin is the watershed draining to the Great Lakes, and the Mississippi River watershed is the continental area draining into the Mississippi River. But what's an airshed? Air is driven by a complicated set of forces having little to do with gravity or terrain. Ocean storms spawned off Africa's east coast end up pounding the United States, Mexico, or a tropical island. Jet streams take a notion, and suddenly Canadian arctic air penetrates the plains or the Great Lakes. National weather typically moves from west to east, but frequent warm southwesterly winds move hot air and moisture up from the Gulf of Mexico for days at a time. How do you define an airshed, and what would it have to do with POPs? I looked forward to the EPA presentation.

The EPA scientist ran through the history of regulation under the Clean Air Act, and how the EPA focused upon automobile and power-plant emissions in the early days.

"We went out to control smog- and ozone-forming chemicals," he said. "The automobile's carbon monoxide and unburned fuels, along with power plants' sulfur oxides, carbon monoxide, and oxides of nitrogen, were our major focus. Once we had achieved the degree of control we thought would impact smog and ozone, we evaluated our progress."

"And you didn't control the smog and ozone," an environmental member said.

"Right," the speaker agreed. "We were successful in reducing emissions, but did little or nothing to achieve our goal of smog and ozone elimination."

"You've bled us dry," a power-company executive said, giving the presenter a stern look, "so what's next?"

"We surveyed several industries and found that millions of tons of hydrocarbons, chlorinated hydrocarbons, and other volatile organic compounds, VOCs, are emitted into the atmosphere annually."

"Where do these come from?" an environmental member asked.

"Paint booths, dry cleaners, bakeries, breweries, refineries, steel mills . . ."

"And pharmaceutical chemical manufacturers," I said, realizing where he was going. The whole group knew Upjohn's chemical plant was the largest VOCs emitter in the state, and that we were installing new control technology as fast as we could.

"Most any industry uses solvents and emits them as VOCs," the presenter said. "Even the high-tech and supposedly clean electronics industry emits tons of cleaning solvents."

"If you didn't know that these compounds were creating ozone and smog, how can you be sure they're not creating POPs?" an environmental member asked.

"If this blanket of chlorinated chemical soup kept the control of power plants and automobiles from reducing ozone and smog, could it also be supplying POPs to the environment?" another added.

"Good point!" a third member said. "Anything could be happening with a mixture of chlorine-containing chemicals in the atmosphere."

The presenter was beaming with joy at the GLRCEC environmentalists' ability to grasp the point. "Exactly our thought," he said, placing a graphic on an easel. "The EPA has designated a list of chemicals as air toxics. This graph shows air-toxics emissions by county for all of Mexico, the United States, and Canada. The U.S. data were obtained from a recent EPA program requiring a Toxics Reduction Inventory (TRI) from all users of the listed air toxics."

The two-by-three-foot graph had vertical bars representing the intensity of "toxics" emissions. It was amazing how much of the emitting industry was close to the Great Lakes.

While we were absorbing his map, he explained that Mexico could be included in regulation because of environmental agreements within the North American Free Trade Agreement (NAFTA). Then he placed a transparent sheet with three potato-shaped rings, like a badly drawn target with the Great Lakes as the bull's-eye, over the map.

"Here's the Great Lakes airshed," he said. "It's defined as the geographical area from which air could transport toxics to the Great Lakes." The irregular circles represented one-, three-, and five-day transport areas. The outside line, the five-day circle, went through Florida, Texas, Mexico, Idaho, British Columbia, the Northwest Territories, and Labrador.

"Nearly the entire North American continent is within the five-day airshed," an environmental member said.

"All the NAFTA membership, anyway," the presenter added.

"And you know how the Great Lakes make their own weather," another added.

"The lake-effect weather would hold the air-driven POPs within the basin like a magnet," another said.

"The EPA is promoting a joint effort with Canada and Mexico to aggressively reduce air toxics," the presenter said. "From initial industrial response to the Toxics Reduction Inventory, we're expecting astounding results."

The presenter was applauded, thanked, and ushered out for the conclusion of the meeting.

"What do you guys think?" the GLRCEC environmental cochairman said, looking expectantly toward the industry members.

I was in shock from the absurdity of the presenter's logic, and devastated by the environmental membership's hook-line-and-sinker swallowing of this bait. I couldn't speak, and the environmental leaders probably thought that I was devastated to find out that our emissions of air toxics were the source of continuing POPs to the lake.

I mulled over the logic. The potato shapes were artificially placed over the Great Lakes, but they could be centered anywhere. This "airshed" nicely included all the political boundaries over which the EPA had any influence. This would keep all the pollution under the control of the USEPA and cooperating regulators in NAFTA countries. The presenter's air all flowed to the Great Lakes and dumped its toxic load there. Did any air flow away from the Great Lakes? And best of all, in an environment where the VOCs are broken down by atmospheric chemistry, somehow these low-molecular-weight compounds are combined to make complex chemicals such as chlordane, DDT, toxaphene, and PCBs. This chemistry was not shown, or expected, to occur in any laboratory or natural setting. This presentation was nothing but a dressed-up version of the erroneous assumption that Pollution Prevention would eliminate POPs.

In the good old GLRCEC days, I would have argued, but the chlorine fight had made constructive argument among the membership impossible.

The great experiment of industrial and environmental leadership in collegial discussion was over—for me, anyway. POPs may transport through the air, but not by emanating magically from air toxics, and within an airshed constrained by political boundaries and centered on an artificial target.

Yet there had to be a source of continuing POPs to support the concentrations in Lake Superior and to keep Lake Michigan and the other lakes' rate of decline so slow that it would be decades, if ever, before they reached Lake Superior's current concentrations. The answer might be blowing in the wind, but how did the barely volatile POPs get into the wind to contaminate the tremendous volumes of Great Lake waters? I needed a reality check at Lake Superior's shores.

LAKE SUPERIOR: JULY 1995

Uncle Reino used a razor-sharp, hand-made butcher knife to separate our catch into fillets and scrap. A large male herring gull guarded his position in front of the scrap bucket with screams and sharp jabs from his beak. A noisy chorus of challengers hovered above the half dozen gulls behind him, looking for their chance to be second at the impending feast. Reino had shared hundreds of catches with them, but their knowledge of the drill didn't increase their patience. I could sympathize with them; the sight of the pink to flame-orange fillets aroused memories of coal-stove-grilled lunches on board the Erkkila brothers' commercial tug and made me wish it was dinnertime.

My favorite part of our annual Fourth of July visit was a return to the lake with Reino or Edwin Erkkila. This morning, Edwin and I left the harbor at dawn in Edwin's sixteen-foot trolling boat, and were back by ten-thirty with our limit of six trout. Reino and I cleaned the fish, while Edwin went home to prepare for the holiday festivities. It was a great day; I got time with both uncles. Fishing with Edwin, using braided wire to drag a three-pound weight at the bottom of a 120-foot trench, was crude but effective.

Reino finished the filleting and dumped the scrap bucket to the screaming gulls. It was time for coffee and, hopefully, stories of the lake.

One fact Reino could not accept was that his lake and his fish were contaminated. "I can see how Green Bay, Chicago, Indiana, and southern Michigan with their farms, factories, and sewage can pollute Lake Michigan," he said. "But what's here?" He swept his arm in the direction of the lake from his front yard. There were a few summer residences near the mouth of the Traverse River, then miles of uninhabited shoreline. "Munising lies 85 miles to the southeast, past the Huron Islands you see on the horizon across the bay. There's 170 miles of lake to the east toward the Canadian shore near the Soo [the locks between Sault Ste. Marie, Ontario, and Sault Ste. Marie, Michigan]. You go 125 miles north to the Canadian shore at Nipigon." He turned to the west. "Across the peninsula, Duluth, Minnesota, is 180 miles away," he continued, and looked me in the eye. "Now you gonna tell me that a few potato farms, some worn out mines, and a few scattered paper mills polluted all that?"

No, I was not going to tell Reino that, and I knew the impending tirade. I'd been there before. Reino was one of the most intelligent and observant persons I knew, but emotion ruled when it came to his lake.

"It's those DNR guys," Reino said. "They catch a fat trout, put it in a blender to homogenize it, then assay for toxics and say the whole lake is polluted. Who eats fat trout?" he said, shrugging his shoulders. "Oh, you can smoke the small ones and they're good, but if they get over two pounds you might as well put a wick in them and use them for a candle. Do you think the DNR guys know a fat Siscowet from a lean trout? We don't eat fat trout, and we clean the fat from our lean trout. We're not getting any toxics. They're measuring fat, organs, and everything."

I knew better, but wasn't going to argue with Reino; there would be no changing his mind. There's not a fisherman or hunter in Michigan's Upper Peninsula, or probably anywhere on the planet, who thinks the "DNR guys" (Department of Natural Resources) know what they're doing.

Siscowet is an Indian name meaning "cooks itself." Their 60 percent body fat may be enough fuel to cook the remaining meat, but it is inedible. To amateurs, like me and the DNR guys, the Siscowet looks like a lake trout.

Contrary to Reino's conviction, the DNR samplers do know the difference between Siscowet and lean trout. To obtain reliable data for determining trends, they take fish of the same size and age from the same spot in the lake at the same time every year. Their fat is measured, and groups of fish are homogenized to obtain a consistent sample. This sampling is done on all varieties of fish for all the POPs in all the lakes. Samples of edible flesh are analyzed for POPs to make the fish-eating-advisory determination. Every year, an extensive fish-eating advisory is issued to anyone buying a fishing license.

Advisories recommend the maximum amount of consumption for various sizes of all varieties of fish. For example, according to Michigan's 2004

Lake Superior guidelines, men can eat an unlimited amount of 26″ lake trout, while women are advised to limit consumption to one meal a month. For 30″ trout, men are advised to limit consumption to one meal per week, and women are advised to abstain from eating any amount. The stated reason for limiting consumption is the presence of PCBs, chlordane, and mercury.

Reino fumed over any limiting of consumption of fish from his seemingly pristine lake. We both consumed beyond the recommended amounts, and he stayed in denial while I rationalized that being past my reproductive years, I could safely enjoy the delicacies Lake Superior offered. However, reading recent research reports about the effect of POPs on the mental functioning of adult males was making the less contaminated whitefish taste better than the trout.

"It's too bad we don't have more people up here," Reino said. "If we had more votes, the governor would eliminate fish-eating advisories and we'd have a market."

"Are the fish back?" I asked.

"Coming back," Reino said. "Whitefish are doing well, but Cecil satisfies the trout market with two or three days of fishing. People are afraid of fish." Cecil, a Native American with an aboriginal fishing license, had bought out Reino's neighbor's equipment.

"In the old days, twelve families made their living from fishing this part of the bay," Reino said. "Now, Cecil's the only fisherman. Lamprey control has allowed the fish to come back, but the governor makes them too toxic to sell."

Many health professionals and activists felt the allowable POPs intake was too high, and were putting pressure on the governor to make the fish-eating advisories more stringent. What was holding POPs in or resupplying them to the lakes? Regulators and researchers were beginning to ask Uncle Reino's question: "How can all that water be polluted when it is surrounded by rocks and trees, trees and rocks?"

Creative research had determined that the majority of POPs were entering Lake Superior through the air. Now it was necessary to find out how they had gotten into and stayed in the air. An air-sampling station—part of the IJC recommended Integrated Atmospheric Deposition Network (IADN)—in Eagle Harbor on Lake Superior's southern shore, coupled with the latest analytical technology, meteorological models, and computers, indicated they were sourced from industrial areas to the south. This started the quest for rapid sampling techniques, improved meteorological models, better computer programs, and faster computers. Researchers hoped to obtain samples in minutes, execute a precise analysis, and when a peak of a contaminant was detected, backtrack it to its source.

In the Great Lakes region, where weather forecasts beyond twelve hours are useless, how could a pollutant be backtracked for two days? To me, this approach sounded like wishful thinking, but serious thought about POPs transport through the air was taking place, and perhaps it would lead somewhere. It was time to expand the airshed beyond the EPA's and Environment Canada's regulatory borders.

EXPANDED AIRSHED: AUGUST 1995

The Great Lakes Regional Corporate Environmental Council tried to keep its lights on, but the ominous shadow cast by chlorine was overwhelming. Honest dialogue among respected professionals degraded to polite tolerance for the enemy. Meetings were canceled, attendance waned, and financial support wavered. GLRCEC environmental and industrial leadership decided to disband and invited old timers to a final meeting celebration. I returned from six months of retirement to commiserate with my old friends and environmental mentors.

In saying our goodbyes, Jim Ludwig, the field biologist, mentioned a project he had been working on at Midway and Sand Islands, 1,100 miles northwest of Pearl Harbor. The Laysan albatrosses were suffering from ingestion of floating plastic as they skimmed the water, feeding on flyingfish eggs normally found attached to floating objects. The albatrosses were loaded with PCBs.

"PCBs in the mid-Pacific?" I asked.

These remote World War II military bases are full of PCBs and pesticides," Jim said. "President Clinton is cleaning them up."

"Didn't you once tell me about PCB contamination in the Arctic?" I asked. "Something about breast milk?"

"That was a Canadian study," Jim said. "PCB levels in milk of southern Canadian women reflected the levels in the Great Lakes, reducing rapidly in the early 1980s and then leveling off. Researchers wondered what a pristine background concentration would be and sampled Inuit women of Broughton Island, north of the Arctic Circle."

"Got a surprise, as I remember," I interjected.

"The pristine Inuit had eight times more breast-milk PCBs than southern women had," Jim said. "It caused quite a stir. Men shunned the women as contaminated. Some babies rejected the powdered-milk substitute and nearly died of dehydration."

"How's the situation now?" I asked.

"It's all right now," Jim said. "They've cleaned up the town's cold-war-era Distant Early Warning (DEW Line) radar base and a nearby abandoned U.S. Coast Guard weather station. The government is telling them to eat the seals, whales, walrus, and polar bears. They're even supplying the Inuit with motorboats, snowmobiles, and rifles to make hunting easier."

"PCBs are sure spread around the globe," I said.

"It's amazing what corporate greed and military muscle can do to the ecosystem," Jim said with a smug twist to his jaw.

I had many unanswered questions, but the GLRCEC chapter was over, and my relationship with a fine friend and excellent field biologist went with it. Jim brought me to my epiphany. He had seen me as "salvageable," and now viewed me as a greedy part of the problem.

I thought of other places where PCBs were found. Some were not surrounded by military might or corporate greed. In the mid-1960s, Soren Jensen accidentally found PCBs in the lakes of northern Sweden. In 1973 a Great Lakes researcher found PCBs in Siskiwit Lake, a lake on Lake Superior's Isle Royale—the middle of a national park. Researchers were now finding elevated levels of toxaphene in high mountain lakes of Italy and western Canada.

Were the birds of Midway and the Inuit of Broughton Island contaminated by the neighboring installations that had been abandoned for decades, or were there other forces busily contaminating sites around the globe? POPs seemed to show up wherever they were sought.

Immediately following the banning of PCBs, levels in U.S. wildlife and waters decreased rapidly, but the concentration in the air lagged. This strange behavior needed investigation. Dr. Ronald Hites, a seasoned researcher from the University of Indiana, sought answers outside the basin.

In the Great Lakes area, summer air was contaminated with nearly a hundred times the winter PCB levels. What would happen in an area of near constant temperature? Historical PCB measurements at Bermuda indicated no concentration trend over a twenty-year period. Was there an analytical problem? Could careful study in Bermuda sort out some answers?

Dr. Hites sampled Bermuda air between the summers of 1992 and 1993 in a study called "Global Atmospheric Behavior of Polychlorinated Biphenyls." Samples were taken from a high tower, and only during appreciable wind to avoid local influence. He concluded that Bermuda PCB concentrations were indeed constant. The only statistically significant concentration deviation was that wind coming from the direction of Africa contained slightly higher levels of PCBs.

The researchers determined that nearly three million pounds of PCBs resided in the global atmosphere. According to their model, the globe was at steady state, with PCBs volatilizing from the water, soil, and vegetation as fast as it was depositing back from the air.

Something seemed wrong with this model. PCBs were degraded by several mechanisms and taken out of the system through deposition in irretrievable locations known as environmental sinks. During daytime hours, atmospheric chemistry worked on PCB destruction through sunshine-induced formation of highly reactive hydroxyl and other radicals. There were several known pathways of elimination of PCBs.

Microbiologists tried to eliminate PCBs from the soils through the cultivation and use of microbes. There was very slow degradation—too slow to be used in remediation efforts, but an ongoing natural process. Animal metabolism was studied, with metabolite products of PCBs found in several species. PCBs found their way into irretrievable sinks such as lake sediments, accumulating tundra, and glaciers.

None of these processes were spectacular in their removal rates, but they went on 24/7/365, and should impact the amount of atmospheric PCBs. With PCB production banned, a decrease in the amount circulating in the atmosphere would be expected. What was keeping the level up?

Environmentalists suspected leaking transformers, illegitimate production, or the continued use and recycling of PCB-containing products, such as old or imported NCR paper. (The original No Carbon Required copy paper that used PCBs as an ink carrier.) These sources were all decreasing and couldn't support a constant global airshed.

Looking toward Bermuda provided valuable knowledge of PCB transport, but a close look at Lake Michigan would provide some surprising airshed insight.

MASS BALANCE: 1996–1997

On retirement, I treated myself to global travel; bought a kayak to probe the quiet waters of Michigan's lakes and streams; did more rollerblading, hiking, and sailing; and took up downhill skiing. Fun stuff, but I couldn't rid my mind of concerns about the recalcitrance of POPs. I stayed in touch with the lakes through Michigan's Great Lakes Protection Fund, serving on its Scientific Advisory Board to evaluate research proposals. The board was an exciting mixture of environmentalists, municipal planners, university scientists, government scientists, regulators, and industry.

Research proposals far exceeded the fund's $2-million-a-year research budget, and the board's diversity led to lively discussions on the merits of each proposal. Past funding had focused on POPs, and there was pressure to follow the trend set by the State of the Lakes Ecosystem Conference (SOLEC) to emphasize protection of habitat and protection from exotic species. Each member's devotion to protecting the lakes proved greater than any difference in viewpoint. We argued with gusto and respect.

"With your interest in POPs, why don't you get involved in the Lake Michigan LaMP efforts?" asked Tom, a federal wildlife scientist, during a break from evaluating research proposals.

"They could use someone of your background," a university scientist added.

"What's a lamp?" I asked. "I'm totally in the dark."

"A Lake-wide Management Plan," the Sierra Club member said, looking at me like he'd always known I was in the dark. "Congress has required a plan for every lake."

"Lake Michigan's ahead of the pack," Tom said. "Being the only U.S. Great Lake, coordination with Canada isn't necessary, so it was funded first."

"The EPA's Great Lakes office in Chicago is pushing the LaMP," the university scientist said. "They're doing a comprehensive mass balance on four pollutants."

"Any POPs?" I asked.

"PCBs," the Sierra Club member answered. "It'll be interesting to really know where PCBs are coming from."

"The Lake Michigan Forum is charged with public input to the LaMP process," Lou, the other industrial member, said. "They need more industry representation."

"I'll give you the head of the Forum's number," the administrator of the fund said.

The Lake Michigan Forum rang a bell. I put it together on the drive home. Mary, the county commissioner who'd heckled me at the Windsor IJC meeting, was doing environmental projects on the Kalamazoo River through the Forum. Since Windsor, I'd chaired a county technical committee for landfill siting, and Mary and I had come to understand each other. She believed in environmental progress through outrage, and I leaned heavily on science, but we could work together. I met her for coffee, discussed the Lake Michigan Forum, and proceeded to join.

My first Lake Michigan Forum meeting was in Kalamazoo to celebrate the cleanup of an abandoned paper mill's waste pond. The next was in Chicago to hear about the mass-balance study.

A mass balance is a basic tool for understanding any system. The EPA defines the term and its use on their Lake Michigan Mass Balance website.

Mass balance is based on the principle of "conservation of mass": the amount of a pollutant entering a system should equal the amount of that pollutant leaving, trapped in, or chemically changed in the system. Determining the amount of pollutants entering a lake via air and rivers, and understanding how they move through the lake and its food web is like piecing together a complex puzzle. The solution to this puzzle is arrived at through collecting environmental samples and then using mathematical models to develop the links between samples. Mass balance is a valuable tool enabling resource managers to design cost-effective strategies for reducing toxic loads and minimizing human and ecosystem health risks.

I was aware of studies of PCB flow into the lake from the air and through the rivers, but there had been little quantifying of the results. I couldn't wait to hear the results of an extensive PCB mass-balance study. I was the Lake Michigan Forum's only industry member present, and the only member with a science or engineering background.

"These results are preliminary," the Chicago-based EPA Great Lakes scientist said, "but there is no doubt the largest vector in the mass balance is volatilization from the lake into the atmosphere."

"It's so bad that the lakes are now a source!" Mary screamed, and pulled her collar over her nose to protect her lungs from the nearby lake. The other committee members drew back in fear.

Amazing, I thought. If the lake was a source of PCBs to the atmosphere now, think of what it must have been fifteen years ago when the PCB levels were seven times higher. I tried to make the point that venting from the lake might have been the reason for the rapid reduction in PCBs for the first few years after the ban, but it was lost in the emotion of their finding Lake Michigan to be a source of PCBs. For these activists, the PCB venting didn't exist until the EPA measured it.

Another amazing mass-balance finding was that transfer from the air to the water was the second largest vector. Both airflows were much larger than PCB input from rivers. It would be several years before the mass balance was complete, but here are the results from data compiled in 1994 and 1995. Results for Green Bay (GB), a contaminated arm of the lake, are reported separate from the main lake (ML).

The amazing finding was that every year, the lake lost more PCBs than were dissolved in all the water of the lake! I did a quick calculation and found

---

LAKE MICHIGAN MASS BALANCE FLOWS (kg/yr), 1994–95 Average

PCBS INTO LAKE MICHIGAN		PCBS OUT OF LAKE MICHIGAN	
Main Lake Gas Absorption	2243	Main Lake Volatilization	3000
Green Bay Gas Absorption	70	Green Bay Volatilization	502
Green Bay Tributary Loading	220	Sediment Burial	349
Main Lake Tributary Loading	126	Export to Lake Huron	‹1
Atmospheric Deposition	216		
Totals	2875		3852
Net			977

Source: From http://www.epa.gov/glnpo/lmmb/results/loadpcbs.html.

TOTAL PCBS IN LAKE MICHIGAN (kg), 1994–95 Average

In Water Column	690
In Active Sediment*	7071

*the top 3 cm (1.3") of the lake bottom

Source: From http://www.epa.gov/glnpo/lmmb/results/loadpcbs.html.

---

the reduction of PCBs in the water column and active sediments to be about 10 percent, a reasonable agreement with the annual rate of reduction of PCB levels in the water column.

The first thing to realize about these numbers is that they are approximate. It is very difficult to estimate flows of PCBs between the air and water in a 300-mile-long, 923-foot-deep lake of differing temperature and contamination levels, but a lot of money and great care went into making these data the best numbers possible.

The EPA personnel and environmentalists focused on the tremendous amount (7071 kg) of PCBs in the active sediment, a term they use to describe particulates in the water, but not consolidated into the stable lake bottom. This material could move with storms, prop wash, and currents until it found a permanent residence and became part of the PCBs buried in stable sediments (349 kg/yr.)

Other studies had found strong circulation currents in deep waters. Fear was expressed that the currents were now stirring up sediments. Again, discovering the currents didn't turn them on; the currents had been there since the retreat of the last ice age. There were more PCBs in the active sediment than in the water because PCBs like to adsorb to particles. PCBs are hydrophobic: they are not like, and do not like, water.

To me, the amazing part of the data was the desire for PCBs to escape from the lake and into the air. PCBs' low volatility—the boiling point of a PCB congener would be in the 350° centigrade range compared to water's 100 degrees—was more than compensated for by its hydrophobic nature. PCBs and all POPs prefer to reside in fat, be attached to a particle, or escape into the air. They don't like water. Green Bay, with its higher level of contamination, had a volatilization to adsorption ratio of 7.2 (502/70), while in the main part of the lake the ratio was 1.3 (3000/2243). The volatilization ratio for the more contaminated part of the lake was 5.5 times that of the main lake. How is this happening? Let's do some experiments.

The relationship between PCB concentrations in air and water in contact with that air is controlled by the laws of physical chemistry. If a small amount of PCBs is added to a gallon jug half filled with water and vigorously shaken, the PCBs will distribute between the air and the water. If kept at a constant temperature and shaken and analyzed repeatedly, the concentrations will remain the same. The water and air concentrations would be "in equilibrium," with the rate of transfer of PCB molecules from air to water exactly equal to the transfer from water to air. If an amount of PCBs equal to the initial amount were added to the jug and shaken to equilibrium, providing the solubility of PCBs was not exceeded, the water and air concentrations would now each be twice their initial levels.

Should the air in our jug be replaced with PCB-free air and again equilibrated, the amount of PCBs in both the air and water would be reduced because of the PCBs that left the jug in the contaminated air. The ratio of PCBs in air to PCBs in water would remain constant as the concentration of both decreased. Repeated replacement with PCB-free air and equilibration would slowly diminish the concentration of PCBs in the water.

If we equilibrate water, air, sediment, and PCBs in our jug, the water and air will have the same relationship as in the experiment without sediment. The PCB concentration in the sediment will be proportional to the PCB concentration in the water. (This assumes that sediment is homogenous. True Great Lakes sediments contain a diverse mixture of particles with various attractions for PCBs. As sediments age, the PCBs migrate to increasingly tight-holding sediment particles. For a given PCB concentration in water, aged sediments will contain higher concentrations of PCBs than fresh sediments. For explanatory purposes, homogenous sediment is assumed.) If we repeat our experiment of exchanging the air for fresh air, the PCB concentration in air, water, and sediment will reduce with each step, but the reduction will be much slower because of the necessity for the incoming fresh air to remove PCBs from the water and the sediment.

If we remove the sediment and flush the air with air containing a constant amount of PCBs, the water will equilibrate to its level corresponding to equilibrium with the contaminated air. If we add uncontaminated sediment to the jug and continue flushing with contaminated air, the sediment will contaminate to a level that is in equilibrium with the water that is supplied PCBs from the air.

While the EPA presenters and the environmentalist members of the Lake Michigan Forum lamented the lack of sediment-dredging funds from a stingy Congress, I focused on what looked like a more formidable roadblock. The waters of Lake Michigan were approaching the PCB concentration that was in equilibrium with the air. If the lake was reamed and cleaned of all sediments and somehow the PCBs in the water reduced to zero, the air would pour PCBs into the lake at an astounding rate. The 7,000 kilograms of PCBs in Lake Michigan's active sediments are a fraction of a percent of the amount circulating in global air. By working 24/7/365, the big air machine would re-equilibrate the lake, with negligible loss to its inventory.

If Lake Michigan was not reamed and cleaned, it would still come to the stable equilibrium with its surrounding air. It hit me like a bolt of lightning. I feigned the need for a bio-break and bolted out of the meeting to avoid showing a face of glee while the environmentalists agonized over their sediments. Once in the hallway, I whistled a loud "Eureka!". That's where Lake Superior is now! It's in equilibrium with the air, and no matter what we do to its sediments, people, or industries, the POPs in the air will control the POPs levels in Lake Superior. Air concentration will control the PCB levels in all the lakes once their excesses are vented. Lake Michigan would end up at a higher-equilibrium PCB concentration than Lake Superior because it is bathed by warmer air carrying higher amounts of PCBs. Eureka. Now, how do we get the POPs out of the air?

The mass-balance discussion was wrapping up a question-and-answer session when I returned to the room. I listened to the concerns about not accounting for the PCBs removed by fishermen. I was more concerned about not including the amount metabolized by the lake's biological populations, from microbes to trout.

"There have been studies on the metabolism of PCBs in several species," I said. "I know it's slow, but with the amount of life in the lake, would it be significant?"

"We've done the calculations on this," an EPA scientist said. "The largest numbers we could estimate were a small fraction of the tributary load," he said. "We decided to put our available money and time on better air numbers."

"Thanks," I said, in total agreement with his approach.

"PCBs are going into the air from Lake Michigan's northern reaches, but here at the southern end, the region is a source to the lake," the chairlady said. "We'll report on studies of PCB releases from the Chicago area at our next meeting."

I met the EPA person who'd presented the mass-balance study in the hallway outside the meeting room. "Thanks for the interesting presentation," I said. "Where do you think the continuing supply of PCBs to the air is coming from?"

"The lake and its sediments are major sources," he said. "You'll hear about regional sources next time, and there are still the industrial toxics emissions."

I wasn't about to enter the Pollution Prevention argument. "How about the air itself?" I asked. "The Bermuda study and others indicating a constant recycle of PCBs through the atmosphere? Won't they continue to keep the lake in equilibrium?"

"The EPA views current global recycle data as suspect," he said curtly. "There are plenty of regional sources. You'll see that at your next meeting."

The mass-balance study was a fine piece of research. For me, it clarified things I suspected but didn't understand. Uncle Reino was right. His Great Lake was not polluted by a few worn-out mines and potato farms; it was polluted by the wind that slapped the waves onto his shore. But how was this air being supplied with a sustained source of POPs? The EPA didn't want to consider global air, but it sure looked like a possibility. I'd have to wait for their explanation of regional sources.

REGIONAL SOURCES: 1997–1998

Air deposition of PCBs from Chicago air to nearby Lake Michigan waters was of major interest to the Lake Michigan Forum. An estimated 20 percent of air-supplied PCBs to Lake Michigan went into the southern tip of the lake. PCB levels of Chicago air were compared to levels in a small agricultural town, with the finding that Chicago air contained three times the PCB concentration. Another study used a highly sensitive mobile PCB sniffer to find increased PCB levels in air near an old power-company transformer storage area. Previous studies had shown the indoor air of older buildings to have ten to a hundred times the PCB concentration of outside air.

Lake Michigan Forum members were astounded by the inside air values and the contribution of a metropolis to Lake Michigan's PCB loads. What about Milwaukee? It probably made a contribution too. A study of Milwaukee was suggested.

The high PCB concentrations in the air of older buildings comes from historical uses of PCBs. Near the end of PCBs' life, 40 percent of them went into construction materials. These paints, fluorescent lamp ballasts, caulks, and extenders in plastic insulation were bleeding out of their host materials as they "dried up" and escaped into indoor air on their way to outdoor air.

In preparation for the meeting, I looked up studies of large cities. PCBs in London and Stockholm had been measured, with the British and Swedes concluding that the problem was decreasing and would continue to decrease. They paid it no more heed. PCBs in Chicago air were down significantly from earlier studies, but the USEPA wanted further study of Chicago and other Great Lakes cities.

I didn't speak up at many Forum meetings, but I couldn't stomach this approach. What would they do to solve the problem, landfill Chicago and Milwaukee? Old PCBs in construction materials and transformer storage lots were a decaying problem. The air was being supplied by a constant source of PCBs. Study of a small and diminishing problem that could not be solved was not a long-term solution. Maybe I'd do better at the Great Lake Protection Fund's Scientific Advisory Board.

I thumbed through the package of two-page research pre-proposals sent for evaluation. Along with a couple of dozen proposals to investigate different POPs in previously unstudied species, find a microbe to remove PCBs from sediments, or develop a biological indicator that would reflect all POPs in the environment, there were a few novel proposals.

A request to study toxaphene in the North Channel of Lake Huron piqued my interest. Another looked at the reported emissions of PCBs from cement kilns, and environmental justice. It proposed modeling the reported emissions of cement kilns to receptor areas, and correlating the PCB deposition with disease rates in the area to determine if minorities suffered in an inequitable manner. One proposal to study PCB concentrations in Detroit air brought a chuckle. The board will kill that, I thought.

The book *Our Stolen Future,* coauthored by Theo Colburn and introduced by Vice President Al Gore, was published in 1995. It blamed trace levels of POPs in the environment for everything from decreased human sperm count to prison overload. This created interest in birth defects and learning disorders, spawning half a dozen proposals.

With my newly gained realization that POPs would be with us as long as winds blew, I looked for research ideas leading to a solution—instead of continually defining more problems with existing levels of POPs, or searching for new problems at lower levels. There were none.

I found the cement-kiln proposal especially repugnant. Cement-kiln owners made mandatory annual reports of the PCB content of their discharges, and a small amount was indeed emitted. I wondered if it would be less than the amount of PCBs in the kiln's air supply, yet this researcher would take that small difference, use uncertain meteorological models to land PCBs in backyards, and see if minorities or other disenfranchised segments of the population were being unfairly harmed. How could anyone sort out the load of PCBs in a person's diet and the indoor air quality from a small perturbation in air circulating tons of PCBs? The proposal contained the attention-grabbing buzzwords of PCBs, modeling, polluting industry, and environmental justice, and would certainly yield an uncertain and faulty connection to some disease . . . and the flaky results would be used to seek extra money for a more definitive study. This was a setup for environmental injustice against the cement-kiln operator. I went to the Scientific Advisory Board meeting with an attitude. Nobody was looking for a cure to anything but their research budgets!

When preliminary rankings for the proposals were tallied, the cement-kiln proposal would have been number one without my zero, and the measuring of PCBs in Detroit's air would have been in the top five. I was out of my element again.

"Looks like you're up, Mel," the facilitator said. "What's wrong with the cement kiln?" I was eloquently negative and managed to sway the vote. Even though the Great Lakes Protection Fund had sponsored a study on seasonal variation of PCBs in Michigan's air, the members could not relate to air as having an ever present background of PCB contamination.

The Sierra Club member championed the study of Detroit's air. I went through the history of decay with time in Chicago PCB levels and the attitude in London and Stockholm, and then asked if landfilling Detroit would take place if the levels were as high as expected from the results in other major cities. There would be no Detroit study.

I do not like being negative, but I was looking at a lot of POPs-related proposals that would do nothing positive. Air was in control of POPs levels in water, and the air was being bankrolled from some gigantic POPs bank. There were no proposals looking for that bank. I supported research on the basics of transfer of PCBs between water and air over Lake Superior, and on several habitat issues. The toxaphene study in the North Channel had been pulled because it was too politically charged. I'd hoped to find out why.

During breaks, I tested my findings of air as a POPs supplier to the lakes on several researchers and scientists. "Was there a global source of POPs?"

I asked. "Are countries outside of North America still using them? Can they get back to us?"

They looked at me like I was from another planet.

"POPs are not volatile; they won't travel that far."

"All major countries have banned POPs."

"That Bermuda study is full of holes."

"Nobody would fund research on foreign use of POPs."

"We can't control others' actions."

"There are enough local problems to cure before pointing fingers."

The movement of POPs through global air was the piece of the puzzle that worked for me, but it wasn't a fit in this crowd. I found out why as I walked to the parking garage with Larry, a retired professor serving his last term with the board. His expertise as a researcher was the behavior of POPs in sediments. He'd been quiet while I was presenting my global-air theory.

"It looks like you may have a plausible theory," Larry said. "It's a fit with the Lake Michigan Mass Balance and the way POPs show up wherever they're measured."

"I didn't get a lot of support back there," I said.

"You won't."

"Why not?"

"They can't afford to."

"Why not?"

"Politics."

"What's politics got to do with this?" I shouted. "I'm talking science."

"The Great Lakes Protection Fund we advise is money generated by individual states; but who supplies the majority of funding to researchers on our board?"

"The EPA."

"Does the EPA want the lakes to be contaminated by foreign sources?" Larry challenged.

"Not any more than by us, I guess," I stammered, wondering what he was getting at.

"The EPA wants contamination to come from sources it can control," Larry said. "If any of these guys talk about the majority of contamination coming from a source the EPA cannot control, they'd better not look to the EPA for future funding."

"That kind of politics," I said, thinking of the EPA's focus on the smidgens of PCBs coming from Chicago, and their lack of willingness to talk about global airflow.

"Do you know why the Sierra Club promoted the Detroit study?" Larry asked.

"Believed it was a major source, I guess."

"You are naive," Larry said with a warm chuckle. "The labeling of Detroit as contaminated would bring outrage, media coverage, excited citizens, more members, and funding for PCB projects. Compare the media attention the Chicago air study got to coverage of real science like the Mass Balance."

"I guess I really am naive," I said. "Maybe I should study politics."

"Stick with science," Larry said. "You've got some good thoughts. Keep at them."

I offered my hand as he turned to his car. "Thanks loads; I really appreciate your insight."

"Are you aware of the upper-lakes toxaphene-contamination flap?" Larry asked.

I shook my head.

"You should be," he said. "It may have global connections. Nothing else fits."

He handed me a folder from his briefcase. "This will explain it," he said, stepping into his car. "Keep up the good work."

I was no toxaphene expert, but in the past two years I'd had a couple of strange encounters with her. She's a real beauty of a POP.

TOXAPHENE IN LAKE SUPERIOR: 1998

The folder Larry gave me as we left the Great Lakes Protection Fund meeting contained several research papers and a conference report on toxaphene levels in northern Lake Michigan and Lake Superior. I thumbed through them before starting my drive. They looked interesting, and I wondered how I had missed such an exciting chapter of Great Lakes POPs controversy.

I refreshed my memory of previous divergent toxaphene encounters on my drive home. Maybe they would come together. Historically, I had not given toxaphene much thought, and had considered it a Southern cotton pesticide and eradicator of trash fish. A Kalamazoo-area lake had had its carp eliminated in the 1960s, and was now the only musky water within hundreds of miles. Toxaphene couldn't pose a long-term problem if you could kill fish with it and then replant the lake after a short wait. Could it?

Just before retirement in 1995, I reconnected with a friend I'd met early in my career. Darrel was a technical salesman I got to know through a complex work project, and after twenty years had passed, I saw an announcement of his promotion to chief operating officer of a New Jersey chemical company. A call to him before a trip to New York resulted in directions to his house on a Connecticut bay and an invitation to fish Long Island Sound.

We got reacquainted over beer and grilled tenderloin. In the *How ya doin's*, Darrel was doing fine. He'd soon be chief executive officer, and the company was on a growth tear, making high-tech chemicals to supply the rocketing fiber-optics and electronics industries.

My career *How ya doin'* was on the wane. The technical challenge of cleaning up the environment for a major corporation was fascinating, but a negative to the corporate coffers, and I was tiring of being perceived as a drag. Head of environmental compliance was a dead-end position, and sixteen years would be enough. The trip to New York didn't help.

In the process of voluntarily cleaning up a 5,000-gallon carbon-tetrachloride spill into a Puerto Rican aquifer supplying two neighboring villages, we had invented soil-cleanup technology that was now being used worldwide. Our rapid response had nearly cleaned up the aquifer. We were looking for an end, and the EPA sent us back to the beginning. They could not accept work they did not order us to do. For them to recognize our effort, studies to their specifications by a contractor of their choosing would have to be conducted.

If we had waited for them to tell us what to do, we'd never have had a chance to catch the contaminant in the fast-moving, limestone-cave-ridden aquifer. Because we volunteered and acted quickly, we would now pay their favorite consultant for a half-million-dollar study to critique our efforts and find more to do.

"Been doin' better," I said, after summarizing my earlier career moves. "Now, every year brings 10 percent more work and 10 percent less satisfaction. Think I'll check out in a couple of years."

"Keep us in mind when you do," Darrel said. "We could find a challenge or two for you." During the early morning fishing trip, Darrel asked if I knew much about toxaphene.

"Just its fish-killing and cotton-insecticide uses, and that it's made from camphor oil," I said. "It's banned now, isn't it?"

"Banned here," Darrel said, "but China needs it badly for their growing agricultural business. Their pesticide use is skyrocketing."

I was somewhat aware of the Asian Green Revolution. A chemist friend was raised on an Iowa farm that was now suffering from low demand and prices because North American exports had diminished.

"We're building a plant in China," Darrel said.

"A toxaphene plant?" I asked, turning to concentrate on the trolling lines to hide my look of shock.

"Can't make it here, and they need it," Darrel said. "New technology using a turpentine cut as feed stock makes the cheapest and most effective pesticide on the planet. It's a great business opportunity."

"But its health and environmental effects . . . ," I said. "Is it really a good idea to get into this?"

"There's no proof of human cancer, and if it affects a few birds, the Chinese don't care," Darrel said. "It's a small price compared to starving."

"What if it doesn't stay in China?" I said. "There's growing concern that the POPs travel through the air."

"Our read is that when toxaphene evaporates, it'll adsorb to particulates in the air," Darrel said. "Particulates leaving China would fall into the ocean and sink to be part of the sediment. It's a geological process that's been going on for eons."

"Oh," I said, marveling at how COOs became CEOs via simple and decisive logic.

"It's only the enviros like the gang you just visited in New York who banned toxaphene," Darrel said. "It's a perfectly good product."

After the encounter with Darrell, I ran into contradictory input. Early in 1998, the EPA Chicago region sought industrial technical membership on committees seeking public input to policy examination. As a retired engineer interested in POPs, I was invited to and attended an EPA pesticide-committee meeting. Since February 1997, the United Nations Environmental Programme, UNEP, had been working on a binding agreement to reduce and/or eliminate POPs. This EPA committee was providing input to the U.S. State Department negotiators.

At my first meeting, the committee chairman reported on his trip to a UNEP meeting and a global POPs-use inspection tour. What a resource, I thought: someone who actually went to China, India, and Africa to get a first-hand look at current pesticide use in developing countries.

"Was anyone making and using toxaphene?" I asked.

"Nobody," he said. "It wasn't being used by any country visited, or by any of the 108 countries involved in negotiating the agreement."

"Not even China?" I asked. "It started from their camphor roots."

"Nothing," he said with confidence. "I talked to their farmers."

"Could they be using toxaphene under a different name?" I asked.

"Impossible," he said. "We had scientific interpreters with us."

"Fantastic," I said, even though I was skeptical. How would banning an effective pesticide—something that took a fight to the Supreme Court in the United States—take place voluntarily in a developing country?

I checked his story in UNEP negotiation-progress publications. Indeed, this was the official word: toxaphene was no longer in use in the world. Fantastic!

Communication with the U.S State Department coordinator of UNEP negotiations confirmed the publication. There was no longer toxaphene production on the planet, not under any name or by any country. Did Darrel feed me a line about his building a toxaphene plant in China? Why would he?

The exercise of recalling toxaphene encounters on my ride home refreshed my memory of yet another incident. On a 1997 trip to Lansing, Michigan, I had run into another old friend with toxaphene insight. Adam was an analytical chemist who'd helped us through problems with false-positive dioxin in our drinking water. We met for lunch. While catching up, I found he was into research on the new generation of pesticides and their life in the environment. Modern pesticides were used at one-fortieth of the loading per acre of the old POPs, and were sold as not persistent, but he could still measure traces of them in the environment. He was evasive concerning the purpose and funding of his research, but proud of his part-per-trillion and below analytical capability.

I wondered if Adam was working on the biodegradation of the current pesticides to make sure they didn't end up on the UNEP's ban list. Adam was a tough researcher. If hired to do something, he did it, and did it well and with scientific integrity. He could not be bought, but he also would not talk about work in progress. I'd probe into toxaphene to see where reality stood on the scale of my two divergent inputs. Was it in common use or voluntarily banned?

"Ever done any work on toxaphene?" I asked.

"As little as possible," Adam said. "Source material or process variations are constantly changing the mix of its 670 chemical constituents. It's even difficult to get people to agree on an appropriate analytical process."

"Is it really on the increase in the northern Great Lakes?"

"It's really there," Adam said. "In my opinion, the historical analytical work is too inconsistent to say what the trend has been."

"How'd it get there?" I asked.

"Not from the paper companies," Adam said. "I didn't do the work, but I reviewed their investigation and it's flawless."

"Could it be coming from foreign sources?" I asked.

"What would make you think that?" he said, with a hard penetrating stare.

"It's in mountain lakes from Canada to Italy at much higher concentrations than in lower-level lakes at the same latitude," I said. "It seems to seek out or survive in clear, cold water. The northern Great Lakes are clear and cold."

"A reasonable thought," he said.

"Could toxaphene still be used in significant quantities?" I asked.

"You could be onto something," he said as he picked up his check and left for the cash register. "Toxaphene is probably the most widely used pesticide on earth," he mumbled in my ear on his way out.

I couldn't wait to get home from Lansing and into Larry's toxaphene folder. I wanted to close the gap between my divergent inputs and understand the current arguments.

A quick look through the folder defined the basic problem: banning toxaphene had not decreased toxaphene levels in fish of the northern lakes. The province of Ontario was issuing more fish advisories for Lake Superior than any other of its Great Lakes, and toxaphene was the reason. One study reported that between 1982 and 1992, Lake Michigan lake-trout toxaphene levels went from 5 to 1.5 parts per million, Lake Huron from 5.4 to 2.4, and Lake Ontario from 4.5 to 0.5, while Lake Superior went from 4.9 to 6.7. Governors and prime ministers didn't like issuing fish-eating advisories and branding their states and provinces as toxic. Answers were needed.

LAKE-TROUT TOXAPHENE LEVELS in Parts Per Million, 1982 and 1992		
	1982	1992
Lake Michigan	5	1.5
Lake Huron	5.4	2.4
Lake Ontario	4.5	0.5
Lake Superior	4.9	6.7

Environment Canada, the Ontario Ministry of the Environment and Energy, and the U.S. Environmental Protection Agency sponsored a workshop, "Toxaphene in the Great Lakes: Concentrations, Trends and Pathways," on 27–29 March 1996. A blue-ribbon panel of university researchers, government scientists, and regulators were gathered to discuss a series of questions posed by the government agencies.

Considerable work had been done on toxaphene, and scientists agreed that deposition from air was the major source to the Great Lakes. There was not an acceptable explanation for greater amounts in Lake Superior and northern Lake Michigan. Three possibilities were considered. First, it could be that the measured species, lake trout, grew faster in the lower lakes, and in a comparison of equal-sized fish, the Lake Superior fish were twelve years old and Lake Ontario's only four. The Lake Superior fish would have been exposed to toxaphene levels prior to its banning.

The second possible reason for Lake Superior to hold onto its toxaphene could be its physical properties of being colder in the summer, deeper, and having a lower sedimentation rate. Perhaps toxaphene was removed faster from the lower, warmer lakes because of their higher concentrations of nutrients, biota, and sedimentation. The third choice was the possibility of a continuing source of toxaphene to the upper lakes.

Historical data existed, but were insufficient to determine which of the three possibilities was most likely. The workshop's report on the question of "What is the trend of toxaphene concentrations in air?" could not be answered with any degree of certainty. Concentrations were higher in the southern United States and lower in the Arctic, varied by season, and were thought to have reduced significantly over the past decade, but changes in analytical procedures made that uncertain. The panel could only say that atmospheric concentrations probably hadn't increased over the past ten years, but there were no supporting data. There were minimal data on toxaphene concentration in the water column and sediments.

The best historical data were on the lake trout and smelt collected for the fish-eating advisories. In the past decade, all lower lakes showed a three- to fourfold reduction in toxaphene levels, while Lake Superior remained constant. It was the consensus of the workshop that "it is likely that sources of toxaphene to the Great Lakes other than long-range atmospheric transport have been important."

It was no surprise that the report of the "Toxaphene in the Great Lakes: Concentrations, Trends and Pathways" workshop recommended a shopping list of research needs, ranging from basic physical chemical data on toxaphene isomers and air-water interchange research to the dynamics of the food chain and sediment core sampling. In recognition of the potential for regional sources, a need to "scope out" that potential through rigorous investigation of sediments, fish, and river mouths of tributaries suspected to be a source of toxaphene to the upper lakes was highlighted.

It was the "scoping out" recommendation that generated the political flap. The EPA immediately called for extensive tributary sampling, focusing on tributaries with paper-plant discharges. There was a tightly linked group of EPA regulators and researchers who, according to paper-company scientists, were convinced that toxaphene in the northern lakes came from paper-pulp bleaching. Their logic was straightforward: Toxaphene is made by chlorinating chemicals distilled from pine stumps. Those same chemicals enter pine pulp in bleaching tanks, and chlorine is present in the bleaching liquid. Therefore, paper bleaching makes toxaphene, and the paper companies of the northern lakes are responsible for elevated toxaphene levels.

The paper industry was irate. They'd responded to previous allegations and analyzed their effluents. They were not discharging toxaphene. They would be guilty by association with studies that would last for years, and didn't want the undeserved flak or the expense of defending themselves. They protested to the EPA and the governors of affected states.

I sought out a friend in the paper industry to learn more about their conflict with the researchers, and wished I had not. The argument had gone beyond scientific dialogue to an outright fight. There were accusations of data fudging and lying as industry tried to convince the EPA of its cleanliness while the researchers were certain of industry's toxaphene contribution.

Tidbits of information were coming together. For decades, toxaphene was successfully used as a trash-fish killer in inland lakes. Later, when used in clear glacier lakes, it didn't work, because toxicity remained and fish couldn't be restocked. Researchers reported toxaphene concentrations in mountain lakes of Italy and Canada at many times the levels of low-altitude lakes at the same latitude. Could these phenomena be related?

The workshop report compared the relative PCB and toxaphene amounts in each lake, with the assumption that both contaminants were sourced from the same air and therefore all lakes should have similar toxaphene/PCB ratios. Lake Superior had three times more toxaphene than PCBs, while Lakes Erie and Ontario had four times more PCBs than toxaphene. If PCB and toxaphene deposit from the air in a constant ratio of toxaphene to PCB, then there must be an additional source to Lake Superior or a more rapid removal rate from the lower lakes.

I looked up the environmental fates of PCBs and toxaphene. PCBs were persistent in water, but vulnerable to atmospheric chemistry. The half-lives of trichloro PCB isomers were measured in days, tetrachloro isomers in weeks, and pentachloro isomers in months. Toxaphene was more resistant to atmospheric degradation, but vulnerable in water.

The report's answer to geographical differences in concentrations was a clear west-to-east trend in biota and sediment accumulation rates, and a possible east-to-west increase in water-column concentrations. What could cause those differences? From my sailing and canoeing days, I knew that the lake's physical differences are more consistent from north to south than from east to west. Northern Lake Michigan is more like Lake Superior than southern Lake Michigan. Southern Lake Michigan is similar to Lake Ontario.

Looking at the geographical trends from north to south rather than west to east seemed like a more logical approach. Toxaphene was present in the clear, cold waters of Lake Superior, northern Lake Michigan, and probably the North Channel of Lake Huron if it were allowed to be measured. The report stated that toxaphene concentration was inversely proportional to productivity. The warmer southern lakes, with their nutrient-rich, plankton-filled waters, were the most productive. They could produce trout in four years that Lake Superior took twelve to match in size.

I recalled canoeing Lake Superior's Keweenaw Bay and getting a feeling of vertigo while looking at rocks and gravel twenty-five feet below the surface. The canoe seemed to be suspended in perfectly clear fluids, and it was difficult to distinguish air from water. I contrasted this memory with walleye fishing on Lake Erie, where bright lures disappeared a foot below the surface. The northern and southern stretches of the Great Lakes are different—very different.

Was toxaphene at decreased levels in the productive southern Great Lakes for the same reason that toxaphene disappeared from inland lakes where it was used to kill fish? In terms of its productivity and biota, Lake Erie is certainly more like an inland lake than Lake Superior. Lake Superior is similar to the glacier lake that can't be restocked because it holds its toxaphene.

I was making a case for elevated levels of toxaphene in Lake Superior without considering a local source. Was this reasonable, or was I just picking and choosing what I wanted to believe? With PCBs, and now toxaphene, it seemed that the carrying of POPs to Lake Superior through the air was the main source, but where were they coming from in an amount that would sustain them for decades? In the Bermuda study, the researchers assumed PCBs were recycled through the ecosystem by a supporting airshed. If the powerful atmospheric chemistry of sunlight and ozone was degrading them at a fraction of the rates quoted in the literature, the air must be receiving a tremendous source of PCBs from somewhere.

I received an invitation to a workshop on air policy and research. Perhaps that would supply some answers.

SCIENCE AND POLICY: 1999

An eye-opening workshop, "Atmospheric Deposition of Toxics: Integrating Science and Policy," was held in Chicago in late 1999. The Joyce Foundation–funded project was facilitated by two non-governmental organizations (NGOs), the Lake Michigan Federation, and the Delta Institute. The workshop's objective was to "take stock of the research on atmospheric deposition of toxics in the Great Lakes and the implications of that research by bringing together leading scientists, government policy experts, environmentalists, and industry representatives to discuss the research, the ability to respond with existing policy tools, and the overall issues that need to be considered in order to effectively address the difficult issue of atmospheric deposition of toxics."

I was happy to be invited to this party and anticipated a wonderful opportunity to hear what the best in the field had to offer, to interact with them, and to learn more about global transport. The workshop consisted of four half-day sessions. The opening afternoon and the first morning covered the current status of research and policy, and the second afternoon and morning discussed future directions and plans.

Conference organizers were concerned about the lack of public communication of POPs issues. A reporter from a major Chicago newspaper was invited to come, listen, and write for her paper. She came, listened, and left at the first break. "If you guys want to be heard, understood, and supported, you're going to have to start speaking in English," she said. "I've been listening to your acronyms and twenty-five-cent scientific terms for two hours and haven't understood a thing!"

I could sympathize with her. I was somewhat familiar with the law and the science, and still felt like an atheist at a theology conference. The mix of bureaucrats and researchers resulted in a barrage of technical terminology and unfamiliar acronyms at a machine-gun pace. The reporter didn't return.

The afternoon and following morning sessions provided ample opportunity to meet with experts and regulators at dinners and breaks. By listening closely, I finally got a good understanding of what was driving the research and policy . . . it was a big circle. The EPA had identified POPs as a fundable concern and looked toward the researchers to provide them with direction. Researchers focused their direction on understanding the movement of POPs throughout the Great Lakes Basin and North America, with the goal of identifying sources for the EPA to control. Researchers always needed more money for basic data, better models, and bigger computers. The money was always insufficient because researchers' main product was defining the need for more research—research that would be funded in the next round.

I was amazed by the research needs. Precise physical chemical data would be needed for all POPs and their impurities to determine how they would react in large and small drops of water, on large and small particles, on leaves and decaying vegetation, and how much would stick to Chicago skyscraper windows on a dry day or be washed off on a rainy day. It was necessary to know whether a particle of a given size would bounce off the surface of the lake or be captured by it—for the complete range of particles found in air.

I asked several researchers and regulators how they would differentiate between the POPs from contaminated sites or other sources from the tons already circulating in the air. Studies on POPs in the air and circulating over the oceans were dismissed as faulty or invalid. Follow-up questions were argued back at me in the true academic fashion—silence. I and my ideas were not worthy of discussion upon their hallowed grounds.

An overly excited EPA representative accidentally released a tidbit of global POPs intelligence before clamming up and disappearing. He was the EPA's chief representative to the UN Environmental Programme for the elimination of POPs. In his talk, he mentioned that Russia had negotiated reductions in POPs for two years while consistently denying their use of PCBs. At the latest session, they confessed to using PCBs and their intention to continue. I questioned the speaker after his talk and learned he had a study of the amount of PCBs used in Russia.

"I'd really like to see that," I said, thinking it would give an order of magnitude of use by a major remaining user. Was it enough to sustain a constant PCB level in the atmosphere?

"I've got it right here," he said, reaching into his briefcase. Then he winced as though his shoulder were dislocated. "Sorry—seems I've left it at the office. I'll send it to you." He had to leave the conference immediately for important ongoing negotiations in Washington. I knew I'd never see the Russian study. The EPA doesn't allow foreign chemicals to enter into its policymaking.

During the next talk, I misbehaved. The topic was residual PCBs still in service in the United States, or in storage awaiting disposal. There was grave concern about leakage, evaporation, and transportation through the air into the lakes.

"Why don't we drum them up and send them to Russia?" I asked. "They're still using PCBs."

"We can't allow these terrible chemicals to enter any environment," the EPA manager said. "That would be unthinkable."

"Please think about it," I said. "Russia will make all they need to use, so sending them our residuals will not affect their use; it will only lower their need to manufacture. On our end, we'd eliminate concerns about PCB leakage, or dioxins formed on their incineration. It's a global victory."

The argument did not sell, and the group rushed into the next topic. After that, I was labeled an environmental atheist and ignored at breaks or meals. Late in the session, a state environmental representative and an activist approached me to say they'd thought through my point and understood my message, but they were shocked when they initially heard it. For some reason, if a chemical comes from "us" in any manner, it is much more toxic and dangerous than if it arrives from "over there." Go figure.

During policy sessions, EPA managers expressed their frustration with the recalcitrant POPs. The agency was doing all it could, and POPs were not under control. They were about to unleash new approaches. The Clean Air Act had an obscure and heretofore ignored requirement to conduct necessary research to understand and better regulate complex problems such as the deposition of air pollutants into water bodies. The researchers could not contain their smiles of satisfaction. There would be major funding opportunities in that cookie jar.

The Clean Water Act also offered an unused policy option. If water-quality standards were not being met, states were required to prepare a Total Maximum Daily Load (TMDL) for the offending water body. The maximum amount of pollutant discharge that would allow meeting water quality would be calculated and apportioned among all sources, including air, land runoff, sediment, and direct discharges. The EPA proposed TDMLs for each Great Lake, starting with Lake Michigan, estimating the program would take fifteen years to implement.

I was glad I'd retired. I could not imagine what controls would result from this approach. The lakes were already receiving more than a TDML from the air. I could see carbon filters being added to every air exhaust, and five years later no progress.

The EPA proposed several POPs policy initiatives. They would continue to pursue the Pollution Prevention program to eliminate toxics, identify more chemicals as POPs, and prevent new POPs from entering commerce. There was no mention of support to the State Department in negotiating the UNEP POPs treaty in a manner that would assure the global banning or minimization of POPs.

The insight and inspiration I had hoped to gain from top researchers and policymakers was more than disappointing. Good research was defined as applying high-level scientific thought to define the minutest detail of POPs transport through the Great Lakes environment. The scientists "didn't have enough data yet" to understand the complex issue of POPs transport, and they could not afford to stop to think about the effects of the thick blanket of POPs circulating over their ivory towers . . . that effort would not be funded. This "scientific" approach was eagerly supported by regulators who had more research dollars than policy options.

My breaking point was approached when the gatekeeper of the EPA coffers straightened me out on the sources of POPs. "You know," she said across the table as the group was assembling, "there are many regional sources of PCBs. Chicago indoor air, for example, is a major source to Lake Michigan. This building, for instance, probably has a hundred times the PCB levels of outdoor air."

I was shocked. We were the first group to use this new conference facility. Most of the complex was still under construction. PCBs had been banned for twenty years. How could she think PCBs were concentrating in the indoor air of a PCB-free building? I knew it was not my place to correct her logic and looked to a well-funded researcher standing beside her. She looked to him for assent, he nodded, and when she turned away he shrugged his shoulders and gave me a wide-eyed "Go figure" look.

On a break, a young man with the Wisconsin Department of Natural Resources asked if I had seen a recent article in *Environmental Science and Technology* on global transport of POPs. I confessed I had not and wrote down the reference.

Driving home, the oft-repeated phrase from President Eisenhower's farewell speech replayed through my mind. "In the councils of government, we must guard against the acquisition of unwarranted influence, whether sought or unsought, by the military-industrial complex." We did not listen to Ike, and there was great influence and massive expenditures throughout the Cold War. Had our approach to POPs created an unsought regulatory-research complex that was caught in a web of spending but going nowhere?

After listening to the goals and expectations of the "Atmospheric Deposition of Toxics: Integrating Science and Policy" workshop, I realized Lake Superior was in long-term trouble. The North American approach to science and policy would fund and produce advanced degrees and wealthy contractors, but no reduction of Lake Superior's POPs levels.

The basic approach to scientific investigation was bothersome. The Lake Michigan Mass Balance study was a scientific approach in which a boundary was drawn around a system and all inputs and outputs measured. The regulatory-research complex's approach to POPs was to draw a box around political boundaries and study the flows within those boundaries. Ignoring real flows in and out of the artificial box was a violation of basic scientific methodology. I had to escape from the constraints of that political box and find unadulterated science, if it existed.

OUTSIDE THE BOX: FEBRUARY 2000

It had been decades since I had visited a scientific library. Once oriented to Western Michigan University's physical layout and electronic searching, I found it fascinating and quickly honed in on the reference received at the Air Toxics workshop.

"Tracking the Distribution of Persistent Organic Pollutants" was featured in a 1996 issue of *Environmental Science and Technology*. The Canadian and Norwegian authors critically examined POPs reported in soils, water, and vegetation from around the world. In 1993 they had postulated that POPs moved from their place of deposition toward the poles and deposited along the way according to their volatility. "Global fractionation," they called it. Weather patterns turned each hemisphere into a distillation unit, moving the more volatile POPs to the poles while depositing the less volatile POPs at mid latitudes. This report refined their earlier theories, and predicted where POPs of various volatilities would concentrate on their poleward journey.

Was this believable? Would the relatively nonvolatile POPs really move to colder areas where they would be less volatile? If so, an airshed with the equator as its only border was being defined. One of their most compelling arguments involved alpha-HCH, the inactive but major component of the pesticide hexachlorocyclohexane.

Global distillation theory would predict that this very volatile POP would move from major use points in the Northern Hemisphere's tropical and temperate zones to the Arctic Ocean. The authors measured alpha-HCH concentrations in seawater along the Asian Pacific coast during the late 1980s and early 1990s, plotting them against latitude. They obtained a smooth curve, with concentrations at 80 degrees latitude being fifty times the tropical levels!

Alpha-HCH was racing to the Arctic, while the somewhat less volatile toxaphene was being smeared across northern latitudes. PCBs were concentrating at mid latitudes and diminishing toward the Arctic.

The authors concluded with a policy recommendation: the global elimination of POPs to protect the polar ecosystems. What a refreshing approach compared to the USEPA's policy options. The fresh air of unadulterated science was invigorating. I continued searching for answers.

How bad was the Arctic? Was wildlife suffering? What about the people of Broughton Island who had gone through the PCBs-in-breast-milk scare in the mid-1980s?

The Broughton Island answer was found in a 1995 article entitled "Indigenous Women Consume Greater than Acceptable Levels of Organochlorines," describing a detailed study of the amount and type of foods consumed by indigenous women from two Arctic villages. Broughton Island, an isolated village where Inuit lived from the sea, was compared with a western Arctic Indian village where people lived off the land. POPs content of all foods eaten were measured and POPs intake calculated.

The women were divided into three age groups: twenty to forty, forty to sixty, and over sixty. Dietary POPs ingestion by the childbearing group was staggering. Toxicologists measure the tolerance to chemicals by determining a "Tolerable Daily Intake" (TDI). A TDI is the amount of material per kilogram of body weight tolerated without negative effect. I took the amount of POPs ingested, the women's average weight, and the 1996 Health Canada TDI values to compare the young Inuit women's ingestion to health standards. It was shocking.

Chlordane was consumed at nearly eight times the TDI, and toxaphene at more than four times. Dieldrin and PCBs were each present at near their TDIs, while HCH and chlorobenzene were each at less than half their TDIs, and DDT was present at only 2 percent of its TDI.

All tallied, these unsuspecting aboriginal women of childbearing age were ingesting more than fourteen times the Tolerable Daily Intake of POPs! A toxicologist may cringe at my addition of TDIs. His logic could be that POPs have differing modes of action and therefore are not additive. However, another toxicologist would worry about synergy between two or three POPs and multiplication of adverse effects. I'll stick with the adding of TDIs to make comparisons.

The twenty to forty year old western Arctic Indians ingested a total of only 0.45 TDI of the measured POPs. The thirty-two-fold west-to-east difference was due to the availability of food and the choices made. Inuit ate blubber and fat from narwhal and beluga whales, ringed seals, walrus, and polar bears. These mammals are near the top of the Arctic Ocean's food chain, with POPs bioaccumulated in their fat. The Indians ate caribou, moose, whitefish, and beaver. Since terrestrial animals do not accumulate high levels of POPs from their vegetarian diets and fish are low on the marine food chain, the Indians' diet is well within accepted TDI standards.

I wondered how the Broughton Island Inuit POPs ingestion compared to the most highly exposed mothers in the Jacobsens' study discussed in earlier chapters. These mothers consumed Lake Michigan fish at the peak of Lake Michigan's contamination.

The average Broughton Island woman was getting at least three times the TDI of POPs as those Michigan women found to bear children with learning and reading disabilities. The Arctic Ocean contained much lower contamination levels than the Great Lakes, but while the Michigan mothers ate an occasional fish, a major portion of Inuit diet was fat from mammals that ate fish, or mammals that ate mammals that ate fish.

In 1971, the typical U.S. diet supplied us with 6.9 micrograms of PCBs per day. That led to the banning of PCBs. Broughton Island's twenty- to forty-year-old women were ingesting 44.6 micrograms per day of PCBs. That's 6.5 times as much, and PCBs are only 5 percent of their POPs TDI load.

The amount of chlordane in the Inuit diet was astounding. In the U.S. Agency for Toxic Substances and Disease Registry's "Toxicological Profile for Chlordane," sixteen- to nineteen-year-old U.S. males ingested chlordane at a rate of 0.004 micrograms per kilogram of body weight per day during the 1977 to 1982 peak chlordane-use years. The Inuit women of childbearing age were ingesting 70 times that amount!

I wondered what the trend of POPs concentration was in the Arctic, and if wildlife was suffering. I returned to my library search and found the Arctic to be large, and study of it complicated. Polar bears were highly contaminated, and in the far north, their reproductivity was affected. I judged the first article I found reporting this to be sensationalism, but kept running into more and more scientific references of productivity and lifespan reductions in High Arctic polar bears. The bears to the south were healthy, but the northern bears were suffering. PCBs were measured and blamed, but after seeing the data on HCH concentrations in the High Arctic, it would be interesting to see the content of all POPs in northern polar bears.

In combing through dozens of articles, I did not see a trend of POPs concentrations in the Arctic, but I did get a feel for the problem of obtaining good data. Polar bears store fat for hibernation, so the same polar bear will have a lower concentration of POPs in his early winter fat than he will when emerging from hibernation with POPs concentrated in his residual fat. Females lose POPs through nursing. POPs accumulate with age, so bears with equivalent fat content will be expected to vary in POPs with age. Cubs are highly contaminated when nursing. Obtaining consistent data to determine a trend was near impossible.

I found many articles funded by the Arctic Monitoring and Assessment Programme (AMAP), an effort backed by eight circumpolar nations. Their website offered a published report, which I ordered, but it did not arrive before I left on my first Arctic trip in August 2000.

THE ARCTIC: 2000

ARCTIC EXPOSURE: AUGUST 2000

Somehow, I became an engineer without being able to read a blueprint. I need hands-on experience to gain understanding. The vastness of the Arctic came through in reading research reports and looking at maps—but what was it really like, and how did the people live? Did they want to live there? How did they survive the long, cold, dark winters? Were they aware of the toxics they were consuming?

The eleven-day "Discover the Worlds of the High Arctic," outfitted by Arctic Odysseys departed Ottawa, Ontario, by jet to Iqaluit and Cape Dorset, Nunavut, where we would board a chartered Twin Otter for a circle tour of Nunavut. The brochure identified all travel as tentative and at the mercy of the weather.

Nunavut, five times the size of Sweden, is the aboriginal-controlled Canadian territory carved from the eastern portion of the Northwest Territories. It was turned over to the Inuit on 1 April 1999, and was still in transition during my visit. Inuit, the aboriginals formerly called Eskimos, make up 80 percent of Nunavut's population. Eskimo, a Cree Indian word meaning "people who eat raw meat," is considered demeaning, while Inuit means "people of the land" in Inuktitut, the language of Nunavut. A single Inuit is an Inuk.

Nunavut-owned First Air's 707 flight to Iqaluit, Nunavut's capital, was different. Tasty food was graciously served, and the forward half of the cabin was dedicated to freight. Other than a once-yearly supply boat, air is the only link to remote northern hamlets. My seatmate was a Greenlandic geologist returning to Nuuk, Greenland—our flight's final destination. She briefed me on the potential mineral wealth of Nunavut, from oil and gas to diamonds.

From Nunavut, we took a short commercial flight to Cape Dorset. Cape Dorset, just above the Arctic Circle, gave us a full twenty-four hours of daylight. The dark hotel window curtains blocked out the light, but there was a constant sound of children playing.

"Don't they ever put their kids to bed?" I asked Don, our guide, at breakfast.

"Inuit families who are not tied to a job in government or serving tourists keep traditional summer hours," he said. "They sleep during the heat of the day."

"Heat?" I asked. "It got all the way up to fifty-six yesterday!"

"They're predicting that the temperature will break the twenties Celsius today—that's 70 Fahrenheit. Listen!" he said. The radio program broke from regular programming for a special announcement—a hot weather alert. Temperatures of 20–22 degrees Celsius could be approached. People were warned to drink plenty of fluids and not overexert.

"It could get to 73 degrees," I said. "Just the temperature some people set their winter thermostats."

"These folks are built to take the cold," Don said. "They'll be hurting today."

Johnny, a local carver and businessman, took us by boat to an island where we would hike the tundra, view ancient dwelling sites, and meet for a cookout. Don had pointed out Johnny's house on our walk from the airport to the hotel. Most houses were prefabricated "doublewide"-style houses sitting on metal piles sunk deep into the permafrost. A house directly on the permafrost would melt the supporting ground and sink into it. Johnny's place, a classy two-story custom-built house with dark wooden siding, sat at the edge of the bay.

"See the tent beyond the house?" Don asked. "With all he's got going on, Johnny can't get on the land during the summer, so his family moves out of the house and into a nearby tent. They just cannot stay in a house during the summer."

"They're little more than a generation removed from a nomadic lifestyle," Ben, one of our group, said. "It must drive them nuts to be pinned down."

Johnny's dinghy was a twenty-four-foot wide-beamed hunting canoe with a 35-horsepower outboard. He carefully ferried us in two trips to his anchored powerboat. Docks were impossible in this area of near forty-foot tides. The hike through the tundra and ancient home sites was pleasant. I had been told the Arctic was either freezing or buggy, but in the 72 degrees the only bugs we experienced were butterflies.

At the far side of the island, Johnny had a fire started for a broiled char lunch with sides of rice and snow peas. The food was fantastic, and Johnny treated us to a short walk to view a caribou and calf before the blueberry pie and coffee. We were roughing it.

In the Arctic hamlets, drinking water is brought to homes by tank truck, and other trucks haul wastewater away. I'd seen the wastewater trucks and general trash haulers disappear down a road past the cemetery, and followed them to the disposal site. A wastewater truck pulled up as I arrived and pumped his load of household wastewater into the upstream pond of a series of ponds in a tight valley.

I had seen similar systems work quite effectively in northern Michigan and wondered how they worked in a much colder environment. A closer look showed that the dams had been breached, and the wastewater trickled into the ocean with little retention. Solid trash, hauled by hamlet trucks, was pushed into a pile, where it was burning. Burned-out metal, bedsprings, rusty engines, and steel drums were thrown over a cliff in one isolated area. Except for the plastic, it reminded me of the 1940s dumpsites of my childhood.

Before our flight out, I took an early morning walk to find Cape Dorset's water source. There was an insulated line coming down from the hills, and a French-speaking crew at the hotel told Don they were working on the upper stretches of the water system. On the uphill climb through town, I ran into the town's utilities manager waiting for a ride to work. He was proud of his hamlet and eager to talk.

"Where does the water come from?" I asked, looking further up the hill at a line of towers carrying an insulated and electrically heated line.

"There's a deep lake a quarter of a mile over the hilltop," he said. "It's gravity flow from there."

"No trouble keeping it from freezing?" I asked.

"We've learned," he said. "We don't run utilities under the permafrost anymore."

"I saw a dug-up leaking system in Iqaluit," I said.

"An ongoing and expensive headache," he said. "That's why we keep it simple and truck water in and waste out."

"How'd the wastewater-system dams get broken?" I asked.

"The system was put in last year," he said. "It worked pretty well in the summer. Unfortunately, it became a big ice cube in the winter, and then the rush of water from the snowmelt in the hills above took the dams out this spring."

"Any way to make it work?" I asked.

"Not in the valley," he said. "We're following other hamlets' progress. If there's a more workable system, we'll install it. Meanwhile this'll have to do."

"I've read that Iqaluit is under federal pressure to treat wastewater and install an incinerator," I said. "Do you get that here?"

"Environment Canada would like to see us meet southern standards without the money or technology to do it in sixty-mile-an-hour minus-40° winds," he said, and we shared a laugh. "We're a long way from the fifties, when they got water by melting ice and threw their waste out the door," he continued. "With the TB rate then, a baby had half a chance of being a teenager. As long as there are so few people and so much environment . . . and we keep improving a little . . . we should keep the environment safe."

"It looks like you're getting more people," I said, gesturing toward a large modern office building on top of a small rise. Below it was a cluster of two-story complexes with at least two dozen apartments. They were empty with the windows boarded. "What's that?"

"Nunavut's decentralized government," he said. I waited for more as he gripped his temples with his thumb and forefinger to quell the pain of thinking about it. "It's Nunavut's desire to have qualified Inuit in all government positions and to decentralize functions out of Iqaluit," he continued. "There aren't enough qualified Inuit to fill the jobs, and the qualified ones have adapted to the Iqaluit lifestyle and won't move. We've gotten our infrastructure ahead of the necessary cultural changes."

"Will your job be taken by an Inuk?" I asked.

"On my last assignment, I trained an Inuk to replace me," he said with pride. "It was a small hamlet, with just my wife and me and one other Anglo."

"Would it happen here?" I asked.

"That would be bittersweet," he said. "I'd love to see an educated Inuk learn the job and gain the assertiveness necessary to interface with and manage contractors, but I'd hate to lose our jobs. My wife teaches school, and with our generous northern pay allowances we're saving for early retirement."

He caught his ride from an employee with a well-dented pickup truck. I realized it was time to catch breakfast and the Twin Otter to the High Arctic.

THE HIGH ARCTIC: AUGUST 2000

"Let's get out of this banana belt and head north," Paddy said, heading out of the hotel's restaurant.

"Paddy's the best Arctic pilot there is," Don said. "He leaves his director's desk in Iqaluit a couple times a year to maintain flying status and visit old friends. We're fortunate to have him."

At the airport, Paddy introduced us to the Twin Otter while his young copilot stashed the luggage. The Otter looked like a freight box with a wing welded to the top and a tail pasted to the backside, but it was the Arctic's most reliable transportation. At rest, it pointed upward, supported by two bulbous "tundra tires" and a small tail wheel. The tiny engines hanging from the underside of each wing looked too small to lift the bulky container. Inside, removable seats of canvas and pipe swung down from each side of the box, leaving a narrow center aisle. Pierre, the copilot, used a free-standing step stool to gain access to a side door and stow luggage in the rear, lashing it down behind the seating area. The eleven passengers faced the cockpit door, a step up from the main cabin.

"We can land most anywhere," Paddy said, patting the tundra tires. "But stay flexible, because we're bound to be weathered out of some part of the itinerary. We don't take chances."

I boarded and belted, finding my aisle/window seat to be friendlier than it looked. The Otter definitely favored function over form. With the wing overhead and large windows, viewing would be fantastic.

"Get comfortable," Paddy said. "It's a long way to Resolute."

The Otter rattled and shook through its engine checks, did a short sprint down the runway, and was airborne. The noise subsided a bit, and the unburned kerosene odors faded, but ordinary conversation was impossible. Paddy shouted out points of interest, and Don wandered up and down the aisle with a map and snacks as we headed north.

It was a long and uneventful ride over Foxe Basin to Hall Beach. We didn't go into town, but had a chance to stretch and have a box lunch in the empty airport's snack bar while Paddy refueled.

"Mel, you have to see this," Ben, the senior member of our group, hollered from a public area. I joined him.

He was looking at a two-by-three-foot beautifully illustrated glossy poster extolling the virtues of eating contaminated sea mammals.

Country food contains low quantities of chemical pollutants
These chemicals have never been shown to cause harm to Inuit; they're
    less harmful than cigarettes

Country food provides better nutrition than market food and has spiritual and cultural values

For your health's sake, eat country food.

"What's going on here?" Ben said. "I thought you said the Inuit were getting an order of magnitude more than the Tolerable Daily Intake of POPs. This says low levels. What's right?"

"They are getting a lot," I said. "It's well documented."

"Does Canada have standards similar to ours?"

"They certainly do," I said. "Sometimes stricter."

"We're in Canada."

"Right."

"But there are different standards."

"Appears to be."

"Why?"

"I don't know."

"It says Inuit aren't harmed by toxics," Ben said.

"It says it hasn't been shown that toxics harm Inuit," I said.

"That's different?" Ben asked, projecting a crusty, gruff attitude. Ben was a Yale graduate and had spent his career as an investment banker.

"It hasn't been shown that cyanide is toxic to crusty old retired invest-ment bankers either," I said. "Would you chance it?"

"It's intuitively obvious that cyanide would be detrimental to my well-being," Ben said. "But—"

"Because you think grouchy old ex-bankers are human, and cyanide has been proven to be toxic to humans," I said, cutting him off.

"True."

"Then make the same assumption for Inuit. There haven't been any epi-demiological studies on Inuit, but they're ingesting way more than people who were affected by POPs, and more than what is considered to be a human Tolerable Daily Intake."

"Will there be any epidemiological studies on Inuit?" Ben asked.

"Not with the government attitude reflected in this poster," I said. "I hope the Arctic Monitoring and Assessment Programme (AMAP) study will give some idea of the effects of POPs on Inuit health."

"If they're getting more POPs than the women in the Lake Michigan study, they must be hurting," Ben said as we loaded up for the trip to Resolute.

We stayed two nights in Resolute, with side trips in the Otter to archeological sites and a graveyard of the Franklin Expedition—that ill-fated, all-hands-lost trip to find the Northwest Passage. Nomadic Inuit visited the Resolute area in summers, but it was not settled until the early 1950s, when the Canadian Coast Guard deposited a group of Inuit from northern Quebec on Cornwallis Island. The settlers were poorly provisioned and sheltered. They suffered badly from the cold, starvation, and tuberculosis. Personnel from the weather station and the Royal Canadian Mounted Police worked valiantly to keep the transplanted Inuit from expiring in their plywood huts.

Early reports to Ottawa indicated that the transplanted Inuit were doing well. When U.S. military personnel, including medics, went to Resolute for DEW Line work, they were appalled by the squalor, disease, and death rate. Conditions were improved, and in the late 1990s the survivors received a financial settlement, but not the apology they longed for.

The energy crisis of the mid-1970s brought a boom to Resolute. Paddy told us of the long lines of aircraft awaiting fuel as every major oil company launched Arctic exploratory efforts. Ice-breaking tankers were designed and plans made to find, harvest, and transport Arctic oil. Stories were circulating of oil so sweet and light that in an unrefined state, right out of the ground, it could power engines. From this flash in the pan, Resolute ended up with an excellent airport and hotel for its 250 residents, but the only employment in the area was a lead-and-zinc mine on a nearby island.

From Resolute, we went northeast to Axel Heiberg Island and stopped at a preserved forest on the way to Eureka, a manned weather station at 80 degrees north. The first evening, we hiked tundra fields in the sunshine, watching distant musk ox. The mountains across the iceberg-dotted bay were saw-toothed and snow-covered—beautiful scenery in the low light of a waning Arctic summer. We planned a van tour for the morning.

Morning brought four inches of heavy, wet snow. No van trip; the roads had turned to grease. A construction crew staying in the weather-station hotel were dejected: their short season was over! We hiked the shoreline, the road to the airport, and played some serious cribbage. Paddy worked on First Air's recalcitrant pickup truck.

By morning, the snow had stopped, the runway was plowed, and we flew north to the Ellesmere Island National Park for a hike and lunch. We got to the park at 82 degrees north, but were unable to land in the windrows of drifted snow. At that point we were 2,530 miles from Ottawa. Had we gone that far south from Ottawa, we would have been in Colombia, South America.

The pilots headed south for Grise Fiord, the northernmost Inuit settlement, at the southern end of Ellesmere Island. Winds shearing over cliffs near town had closed the airstrip. We'd have to travel on and stay at our next stop, Pond Inlet, for two nights. Paddy said that Grise Fiord visits were frequently aborted, and he would treat us to lunch at the Coberg Island research station.

Coberg Island lies off the coast of Ellesmere Island, west of Greenland. I wondered how many researchers we would see. The "research station" turned out to be an abandoned portable shack, heavily cabled and anchored to keep it from blowing away, and the lunch was a carry-out of yesterday's roast musk ox from the Eureka weather-station's excellent commissary. The research station had been manned for one winter to study polynyas—areas of no, or very thin, ice existing in the coldest of Arctic Ocean areas. The scientists determined that polynyas were kept open by a constant eighty-mile-an hour wind. For this research, one winter was enough.

The weather was clear and pleasant during our stay. Fog rolled off the glacier-covered hills and the frozen rivers, and chunks of crystal-clear ice clattered in the gentle surf.

At Pond Inlet, I heard of very tempting nature-viewing trips to the ice edge in the Arctic spring. From there, we flew down Baffin Island's east coast for spectacular views of glacier-covered mountains, stopped at the mystical town of Pangnirtung, and returned to Iqaluit.

This trip had more than satisfied my need for a hands-on experience, but I had to come back and learn more about the Inuit, and if and how their incredible ingestion of POPs would affect their future. I was eager to get back to the library and, hopefully, my requested copy of the AMAP report . . . right after I scheduled a return trip to the Arctic.

ARCTIC RESEARCH: 2000–2001

THE AMAP REPORT: AUGUST 2000

On my return from the Canadian High Arctic, the AMAP report, all 859 pages of it, was waiting for me. "AMAP, 1998, AMAP Assessment Report: Arctic Pollution Issues" (Arctic Monitoring and Assessment Programme), published in Oslo, Norway, was a beautiful summary of all the Arctic research I had been finding in bits and pieces. In 1991, eight circumpolar nations— Canada, Denmark/Greenland, Finland, Iceland, Norway, Sweden, Russia, and the United States—established AMAP to examine levels and effects of the Arctic's anthropogenic pollutants. Sponsoring countries, indigenous organizations, international organizations, plus Germany, the Netherlands, and the United Kingdom participated. Data from approximately 400 programs and projects were used. AMAP funded and executed research to fill data gaps where needed.

The AMAP report is clearly written and well illustrated, with four-color charts, graphs, and excellent maps. Extensive references to original work are given with each chapter. The Arctic Monitoring and Assessment Programme is ongoing and maintains an excellent website at http://www.amap.no/. I'll highlight the background and focus on POPs investigations and findings.

AMAP introduces the Arctic's unique physical and geographical characteristics, weather and climate, ecosystems, industries, wildlife population distribution, and human cultures, population, and distribution. This provides an excellent background to consider and study the sources, transport, and accumulation through the food chain of several pollutant classes. Not only is there excellent coverage of POPs, but in addition, heavy metals, radioactivity, acidifying pollutants and Arctic haze, petroleum hydrocarbons, climate change, ozone, and UV radiation are addressed as pollution concerns. The report concludes with a discussion of the effects of pollution on human health.

I dove into the chapters on contaminant transport, people, POPs, and human health. Was POPs contamination in the Arctic getting better or worse? Was the hemispheric airshed a dominant factor in POPs transport? Could Lake Superior be influenced by the hemispheric airshed? Is Arctic wildlife hurting? How many people were getting ten times a TDI of POPs?

One of the most interesting revelations was the geographic deposition of POPs. The most amazing was the previously mentioned transport of alpha-HCH to the Arctic, and how it was fifty times more concentrated in the Arctic Ocean than in tropical waters.

PCBs are much less volatile than alpha-HCH, so they move more slowly. There was a significant correlation between increasing northern latitude and decreasing PCB concentration. Guess what? The concentration of PCBs in Lake Superior's sediments was just what would be predicted from analysis of large freshwater lakes from the Arctic to the Great Lakes. Lake Ontario, with its local anthropogenic influences, had significantly more PCBs than would be expected. Lake Superior was beginning to appear as a lake under the influence of global forces, and relatively unaffected by inputs from within its own basin.

If Lake Superior was responding to global PCB concentrations, it would have to be through the airshed. What did AMAP say about the air transport? Air transport of pollutants in the Arctic was first recognized in the 1950s, when polar-route airline pilots noticed a stable wintertime "Arctic Haze" forming over the Canadian Arctic. The acid rain and heavy metals causing the haze were found to be coming from Russian and Scandinavian smelters and power plants. Two-thirds of the heavy-metal pollutants in the eastern Canadian High Arctic were estimated to arrive on a steady winter wind from the highly industrialized portions of the Russian and European Arctic.

AMAP identified past and current use of POPs in the mid latitudes of the Northern Hemisphere as the most likely source of Arctic POPs. Time trends for any POPs concentrations were difficult to establish . . . except the definite and sharp decline in concentration of alpha-HCH. HCH is the most volatile of all POPs, and the alpha-HCH was an inactive isomer and major component of crude HCH used in developing countries. In the early

1990s, developing countries gained the capability to economically produce Lindane—pure gamma-HCH—and alpha-HCH was no longer manufactured or used. AMAP reported that Arctic alpha-HCH concentrations had greatly diminished since the cessation of its manufacture.

The trend of most POPs concentrations with distance was generally in a north–south direction, such as the previously mentioned PCB and HCH trends. Toxaphene, along with HCH and chlordane, trended toward higher concentrations in the north. The wintertime wind transporting the haze from Russia to Canada left a concentration of dioxin that decreased from northwest to southeast, the expected relationship between a source and wind direction for this POP of very low volatility.

Wildlife at the upper end of the Arctic food chain accumulated POPs at levels capable of impairing reproduction, passing on subtle neurobehavioral effects to offspring, or suppressing immune systems. The AMAP report identified mink, otter, gyrfalcon, merlin, white-tailed sea eagle, and peregrine falcon as species with detrimental POPs levels. Greenland halibut had toxaphene levels suspected to be high enough to affect bone development in their young and result in increased mortality on spawning. The fish-eating seabirds—guillemot, kittiwake, and puffin—were found with PCB levels exceeding reproductive effects. Ringed seal–eating walrus had PCBs at reproductive-failure levels. Walrus, harbor porpoise, several species of seals, minke whale, and narwhal had PCB levels expected to cause subtle neurobehavioral effects in offspring.

On Svalbard Island, north of Norway and east of the tip of Greenland, AMAP described excessive amounts of PCBs found in polar bears, and researchers suspected POPs contamination was reducing reproductivity and survival of young. Svalbard Arctic fox had PCB levels exceeding those expected to cause reproductive and other effects. A trip to the Western Michigan University library provided updated studies estimating 50 percent reductions in the birth rate and life span of Svalbard bears.

Of all the Arctic's human inhabitants, only Greenlandic and Canadian Inuit consume a diet rich in sea mammals. If marine mammals were suffering from POPs ingestion, what was happening to these humans at the next step up the food chain? The AMAP report identified the coastal Inuit as the Arctic's humans in the most danger of health effects of contaminants. Along with POPs, coastal Inuit were found to have extremely high mercury blood levels, with a portion of the population contaminated "above those levels associated with a known risk for neurological damage." In northwest Greenland, Inuit hair samples contained three times more mercury than hair from preserved archeological samples from the late 1400s. The combination of mercury and POPs in coastal Inuit puts their health, reproductivity, and ultimate survival at risk.

Inuit boys born to mothers with high levels of PCBs were of lower birth weight, and as one-year-olds suffered a high incidence of ear and other infections. PCBs were measured in these Inuit mothers, but we need to remember that a high level of PCBs is probably just an indicator of high levels of all the dirty-dozen POPs and mercury. Given the birth weight and immunosuppressant indications, the neurological effects of learning disabilities and attention deficit found in the Jacobsens' work on children of mothers consuming Lake Michigan fish would be expected to be found in Inuit children, and were indicated in the AMAP report.

The report also expressed concern for human reproductive effects and cancer. Most POPs are suspected carcinogens, and suppression of the immune system can make a person more susceptible to cancer. The hormone-mimicking POPs in coastal Inuit are suspected of lowering sperm count, interfering with the development of sex organs, and making it difficult for a woman to become pregnant or carry a fetus to term.

AMAP recommendations focused on protecting people, research needs, and emission reductions. The first priority was to protect people from ongoing exposure to harmful levels of chemicals. AMAP recommended communication of the presence of chemicals in foods, the risks of chemical exposure, and the benefits of country-food gathering and consumption. This communication was to take place in a language and manner understandable to the exposed population. Regarding breast-feeding, AMAP recommended that Inuit continue the practice, implying that the cultural, bonding, and nutritional values outweighed any risks, without presenting backup data to defend that position.

The projected amount of research needed to understand source-receptor relationships and to close data gaps on contaminant trends, levels, and effects was overwhelming. The vastness of the area, diversity of ecosystems, and drastic seasonal changes would require decades of study and exorbitant funding to obtain a rudimentary scientific understanding of source, transport, fate, and effect of POPs, heavy metals, radioactivity, acid rain, ozone, and hydrocarbons in the Arctic environment.

Emissions reduction was recommended through action in the circumpolar countries, and in cooperation with regional agreements. AMAP gave strong support to the United Nations Environmental Programme (UNEP) pursuit of a legally binding global agreement on POPs control and banning. Data presented on continuing global use was sketchy, but the AMAP researchers definitely focused on global elimination of POPs.

Overall, the AMAP report was a thrilling find. The manner in which POPs moved around the world from wherever they were used, to end up contaminating northern and pristine areas, helped in understanding Lake Superior's ability to hang on to banned POPs. Lake Superior was beginning to appear as a part of an overwhelming global system, and no matter what science or policy options were applied to the Great Lakes ecosystem, the PCB, toxaphene, and chlordane pollution of this vast, cold, clear northern lake would not go away.

The personal satisfaction gained by stepping out of the box of North American thinking and finding science that began to make sense of Lake Superior's lingering contamination was tempered by the shocking realization of the effects of Arctic contamination. The top of every food chain was affected by POPs. Land mammals, sea mammals, and birds of prey all had POPs levels that would influence their lifespan and reproductivity.

At the very top of the marine food chain, the isolated coastal Inuit, levels of POPs exceeding the generally accepted TDI by fifteen-fold were being ingested by women of childbearing age. Risk communication, as recommended in the AMAP report, was not being accomplished. On the contrary, Inuit were encouraged to consume more POPs, while very strict standards for POPs and mercury were communicated to people in the Great Lakes region. Not consuming Great Lakes fish is an inconvenience; the people of the Great Lakes Basin can find and afford nutritious substitutes. The Inuit need a supply of alternative nutritious food, not told to eat poison!

I had to return to the Arctic to spend time on the ice with natives. Were they getting POPs education other than the posters I had seen in public places? Heeding it? What problems did experienced hunters see with wildlife health? Were there changes in wildlife populations? A week-long trip to the ice edge at the mouth of the strait between Baffin and Bylot islands was scheduled for June 2001.

While waiting impatiently for this return trip, I researched the history of POPs use. I had expected the Arctic's POPs toxicity to come from PCBs and DDT, the culprits identified as the destructive POPs in the Great Lakes. I was surprised to find that, as measured by their Tolerable Daily Intakes (TDIs), toxaphene and chlordane were the major contributors to Arctic human toxicity. In my recalled history, toxaphene was used on cotton in the Southern United States, and chlordane was a rather minor pesticide used for subterranean termites. Researching the history of POPs provided more surprises.

THE DIRTY-DOZEN POPS

While continued POPs use was being questioned in the United States, I was too busy making chemicals to be involved in the argument. I was aware that a few radicals were attempting to ban PCBs and DDT, but was not directly involved, and I knew that all marketed chemicals were government-approved and would break down in the environment. A mechanic friend, who had been using waste PCBs to clean grease from his tools and hands for twenty years, had not been harmed. Was there any real proof that PCBs and DDT harmed birds? Salesmen demonstrated the safety of DDT by eating a pinch. Wouldn't they be aware of any potential dangers? My attitude at that time was obviously skewed, and I needed to revisit the uses and banning of POPs. I needed a better understanding of their makeup and use rates if I was going to understand how they got to and were staying in the Arctic.

I'll briefly cover their history of use and describe them chemically. More details can be found in the U.S. Department of Health and Human Services' Agency for Toxic Substances and Disease Registry. They have toxicological profiles for all the "Dirty Dozen" and many more chemicals of interest. These comprehensive, 200-page (or more) documents can be found online at http://www.atsdr.cdc.gov/toxprofiles/tp90.html.

Another good source of POPs information is *Chlorinated Organic Chemicals in the Environment*, by Ramamoorthy and Ramamoorthy (CRC Press, 1997).

Of the tens of thousands of commercial chemicals, there are ten pesticides, one industrial chemical, and one byproduct of chemistry that make up the dirty-dozen persistent organic pollutants. PCBs are industrial chemicals, and "dioxins" are byproducts of chemistry and natural processes.

The pesticides are DDT, hexachlorobenzene, chlordane, hexachlorocyclo-hexane, toxaphene, Dieldrin, Aldrin, Heptachlor, and Mirex. All of these highly chlorinated chemicals were introduced as a significant improvement over the products they replaced, and several were sold on the basis of their safety and environmental benefits.

PCBs were commercialized in 1929 to cool electrical equipment such as transformers and capacitors. They were much safer than the flammable mineral oils they replaced. The versatile liquid mixture of chlorinated biphenyls was soon welcomed into use in hydraulic fluids, high-temperature heat-transfer applications, and lubricants. By 1970, PCBs were found in paints, plastics, sealants, caulks, resins, inks, waxes, and adhesives. Non-coolant use accounted for nearly half of the 85 million pounds per year produced and used in the United States.

DDT was a life saver and was known as the chemical that won World War II. The first 500 pounds manufactured was credited with saving 5,000 soldiers from a budding lice-borne typhoid-fever epidemic. After the war, DDT fought malaria-bearing mosquitoes on a global basis and saved millions of lives. Its developer was awarded a Nobel Prize for medicine.

On the farm, DDT was a welcome replacement for existing toxic and persistent heavy-metal pesticides based on arsenic, mercury, thallium, and lead. It rapidly entered our homes, gardens, and neighborhoods. DDT "fogging" trucks sprayed swimming pools, neighborhoods, and parks to rid them of pesky mosquitoes, while children skipped through the welcome cloud of pesticide.

Between 1950 and 1993, an estimated 5.7 billion pounds were dumped into the global environment. When pests mutated to develop DDT resistance, toxaphene and the other POPs were waiting in the wings. Toxaphene took over when DDT was banned, and through 1993, its global usage was estimated at about half that of DDT.

Chlordane and the other dirty pesticides entered the marketplace in the 1940s and 1950s to serve various special applications or to take over from the fallen DDT. They were all phased out and virtually banned when found to have human cancer-causing potential, or to cause direct and disastrous effects on wildlife.

Dioxin is an "illegitimate" POP in that it was never made for commercial purposes. It is formed as a byproduct of chemical reactions and combustion. It is also found naturally in swamps and moist areas. PCBs and hexachlorocyclobenzene can also be created through errant chemistry. Developed countries have learned to minimize the production of POPs in combustion and chemical processes.

When DDT was found to be detrimental to wildlife, and potentially to humans, it was banned; but pests remained. New chemicals were required, and our pesticide approval process allowed the manufacture and marketing of chemicals not acutely toxic to people who manufactured or applied them, or to consumers of products containing residuals. There was no provision for considering the effect of a pesticide on the initiation of cancer, or its interference with the human reproductive system. No wildlife effects or concerns about the use of wildlife for food were addressed.

This pest-management system resulted in the introduction of a series of highly chlorinated and persistent chemicals that did not leave a trail of bodies in their manufacturing or use areas, but spread into the environment to cause subtle and long-term effects on humans and devastation to wildlife. Is it any wonder that the 1991 environmental activists proposed banning chlorine to stop this chain of insane actions?

My review of the dirty dozen astounded me as I found out how "dirty" some of them were and how little is known about their fate and toxicity. Dioxin, known as the most toxic POP, sounds like a pure chemical. A close look shows that when scientists report dioxin concentrations, they also include dioxin's close cousin "furan." The basic dioxin molecule can be chlorinated at eight sites, but the most toxic dioxin is a congener containing four atoms of chlorine and is known as TCDD (2,3,7,8, Tetrachloro-p-dioxin.) There are 75 unique chlorinated dioxins and 135 unique furans. One of "dioxin's" 210 congeners was found to have nearly the same toxicity of TCDD, one has half, and eight have 10 percent. Dioxin toxicity is reported as the sum of the toxicities of all dioxin and furan congeners present, and is expressed as TCDD toxicity. You seldom hear of furans; they are included in the dirty mixture called dioxin.

PCBs are a mixture of 209 unique chemicals obtained by chlorinating biphenyl. Each of the 209 individual PCB congeners has its own physical properties and toxicity. Toxicity of many of the individuals has been measured, with the most toxic being 10 percent as toxic as dioxin's TCDD congener.

DDT is a clean chemical in that it is manufactured as a rather pure solid. In the environment, it degrades to DDE, which is as toxic as DDT.

When concentrations of DDT are reported, they really are the total of DDT and DDE. You may have heard people discounting the toxicity of DDT because its half-life in the environment is only twenty-eight days. True, but it decomposes to DDE, which is just as toxic and very persistent.

Toxaphene is a very dirty product resulting from the chlorination of "technical camphene," a turpentine-like complex mixture of chemicals. The resulting toxic soup called toxaphene is a mixture of 670 different chemicals, many of which are not identified and are of unknown toxicity.

Chlordane is another chlorinated concoction of 140 unique chemicals, of which 120 have been identified. The rest of the POPs are relatively clean, with only a few isomers or a small percentage of impurities.

The "dirty dozen" POPs represent a nightmarish mixture of thousands of chemicals, all possessing unique physical properties, environmental stability, and toxicity. Consider the environmental-degradation products and metabolites of these chemicals, and thousands of new chemicals of unknown toxicity appear in the environment.

The use of highly toxic and persistent chemicals in billion-pound quantities may have been justified to prevent human starvation when "dilution was the solution to pollution," but now we know better. The Arctic is contaminated to the degree that wildlife reproductivity and survival is compromised, and humans are consuming food so toxic that it would be prohibited from placement in a modern landfill.

I had to get back to the Arctic for a closer look. Were the Inuit really uninformed about the toxics in their food? Did Inuit of child-creating age restrict their intake of the most toxic of foods? I called my outfitter and asked him to arrange a stopover in Broughton Island on the way home from the ice edge. If any Inuit would be aware of and sensitive to POPs, the Broughton Islanders should be. It was their high levels of breast-milk PCBs that led to the initiation of the Arctic Monitoring and Assessment Programme and extensive dietary studies of POPs ingestion rates.

RETURN TO THE ARCTIC: 2001

THE ICE EDGE

Last August, two glaciers appeared as slashes of white on Bylot Island's dark mountains across the strait from Pond Inlet, and a lone iceberg was slowly deteriorating just off the shore. We hiked the shoreline and picked blueberries in warm sunshine.

This June, the iceberg remained trapped in five feet of ice near where it was grounded last summer, but the glaciers were invisible in Bylot's snow-covered landscape. On our walk from the airport to town, we saw a polar-bear hide stretched on a frame leaning against a house. Someone took a spring bear with high POPs concentration in its remaining fat. I wondered if he had eaten it and shared it with his children.

We (two thirty-something couples and I) stayed at a comfortable bed-and-breakfast run by the high-school principal and his teacher wife. The Nova Scotian educators had spent several winters in Pond Inlet. What an opportunity to learn about the local educational system's POPs under-standing and teaching. I broached the subject. They had heard of the Broughton Island scare and thought it had been taken care of by clean-ing up the local weather station and DEW Line base. Their belief was that country foods were nutritious, and Inuit should be encouraged to eat them. My questioning made them nervous. I decided to forget about POPs and enjoy a trip to the ice edge, a promised Arctic springtime natural paradise.

At the Sirmilik National Park office, an Inuit ranger of indeterminate age, with his weather-tanned and wrinkled face of experience surrounding youthful bright eyes, made certain we had proper equipment and respect for polar bears. We learned that the hide stretching in town was taken on a special permit to eliminate the hazard of a bear in town.

Satisfied with our preparation, the ranger excused himself for a moment and returned with a four-color satellite view of Bylot Island. "Here's the latest shot of the ice," he said. "Looks like you've got a long ride." We looked quizzically at the unfamiliar photo and the grinning ranger.

"We're iced out of the Pond Inlet end," Dave (our outfitter) said, pointing to the nearby inlet. "A cold snap during a windless night froze the surface for a mile out. It's too thin to travel on, but keeps the wildlife away." He pointed to Navy Board Inlet at the northwest corner of Bylot Island. "The ocean is open here," he said, "right up to the five-foot-thick ice covering the strait."

"Can we get there?" Michael, one of our group, asked.

"Just takes gas and time," Dave said. "I'll get the gas and you get ready for a long ride."

We arrived at the edge in the twilight of an Arctic midnight and pitched our tents near the Baffin Island shore within a half a mile of Lancaster Sound. Six inches of soft snow covered the five feet of ice. I downed a steaming cup of hot chocolate, slid into a puffy down-filled sleeping bag, and slept in toasty comfort until mid-morning.

Later in the day, we snowmobiled toward the middle of the strait and nearer to the ice edge, then up the gentle slope of a trapped iceberg. We hiked up a steeper slope and peered over to gain a spectacular view. We looked down at the edge, with a monstrous Greenlandic iceberg serving as a backdrop. Feeding gulls and ravens focused our attention on walrus carcasses, remains from an Inuit hunt. Within moments we spotted six creamy-white polar bears: a female with two cubs, a large male, and a pair of juveniles.

Conditions were perfect. The wind was in our face, and the bears were far enough away to comfortably ignore us but close enough to photograph and watch through field glasses. We were mesmerized for hours as the female protectively herded her offspring, the juveniles wrestled and cavorted, and the large male was left alone, gorging on a walrus carcass. When the juveniles wandered in our direction and around our iceberg, Dave protectively gathered "his brood" and took us back to camp.

The next day I joined Dave in a kayak and left the camcorder with the cook. We saw two young narwhals right after the launch, but had no more mammal encounters. Our return to camp after an hour of paddling was just like any return from a fishing trip.

"You shoulda been here," Jacques shouted as we approached the edge. "Narwhals were right here at the edge! Dozens of 'em."

"I hope you got pictures," I said as he documented our landing.

He showed us the narwhal pictures—so close you could have thrown them popcorn.

During lunch, Leuty, an Inuk guide, cocked his head and listened. "They're coming back," he said. In a few minutes, we too could hear the blowing, and stood to see the water sprays. A parade of narwhals came in and circled in front of us while they dove for food. We got a good view of their intricately patterned hides of creamy ivory and shades of emerald, but only one "maybe" glimpse of a tusk. This "tooth gone awry" is located low in the head and stays underwater while exposing the back to breathe.

The narwhal left, and someone said, "I wonder if we'll see any beluga?"

On cue, dozens of bright white beluga whales appeared. Six of them liked our area and stayed to feed, rolling in the water and waving their small fins. While our attention was riveted on the ocean, a visitor was approaching from the ice.

"Is that bear a problem?" Lisa said, pointing to a bear loping across the ice in our direction. I was comforted by the sudden presence of Leuty beside me, holding a rifle that appeared from nowhere.

"It's a young male," Leuty said, "probably four or five years old." The bear stopped to look at us. Leuty put the rifle away, stating, "He's just curious."

The bear kept coming. Its feet and forepaws were massive. What a powerful animal. He posed on a pile of ice and then came toward us again.

"I don't think he heard you." I said, with the beautiful bear nearly filling my camcorder screen. Leuty ignored me, and the bear approached within seventy-five yards for a closer look, sniffed the wind, and finally loped away when he heard the distant whine of an approaching snowmobile.

The next day at the edge was bright and sunny. A large, lone walrus skittered away as we arrived. There was a scarcity of pack ice, and the only other mammal spotted was a rapidly swimming polar bear, using the water route around us to the walrus carcasses.

The paucity of mammals was replaced with an abundance of birds. A group of thick-billed murres were feeding nearby. Standing at the edge, we viewed them swimming underwater and captured their surprised looks when they surfaced at our feet. An occasional black guillemot dropped by, and long lines of eider ducks flew the edge in gently rising and falling paths. Kittiwakes hovered in front of us and descended vertically to take some tasty tidbit, attracting a noisy crowd of hungry friends. Long-tailed ducks, northern fulmars, and an occasional flock of long-tailed jaegers flew by.

On the last day, we dangled a hydrophone into the water and listened to the clucks and tunes of underwater life while Leuty and Mathias, an elderly guide, matched sounds to mammals. I enjoyed listening to the Inuit communicate in Inuktitut, using what seemed to be a plethora of guttural sounds interconnected with hums and grunts. Leuty told us that Inuktitut was closer to Japanese than any other language he had heard.

While listening to Leuty and Mathias identify sea-mammal sounds, I wondered about the lack of orcas (killer whales). In researching POPs and the Canadian High Arctic, I had run across two references to orcas, both written in the 1950s. *Spring on an Arctic Island*, a book about a birding trip to Bylot Island, describes finding a beached orca that choked on the twenty-fourth seal he had ingested in a feeding frenzy. In another book, *The Arctic Year*, two naturalists who had spent years in the Arctic mentioned their concern about kayaking near orca hunting the ice edge for nursing narwhal pups. If nursing narwhal pups and baby seals were the orca's major diet, they would be getting a POPs load that would interfere with reproduction. Possible?

"We haven't seen any killer whales," I said, standing with Leuty at the edge and scanning the water.

"Noooummm," he said in a mournful tone.

"Were they once here?"

"Years ago."

"At the edge?"

"Ummm."

"Taking narwhal pups?"

"Ummmm."

"Did you see them?"

"As a boy. . . . Small boy. . . . Maybe my father told me," Leuty said slowly, appearing to sort out if he had seen orca whales at the edge or if he had only heard about them from his father.

"Where'd they go?"

"Away," Leuty said, with a sweep of his arm across the horizon.

This proud man of the Arctic gave the same answer Uncle Reino had given about eagles years ago. Did Lake Superior's eagles and Canada's High Arctic orca whales suffer the same fate?

I worried about another possible fate of the killer whales. Would Inuit hunters view them as competitors for the narwhals and shoot them? I would never get a better chance to ask.

"Shot by your elders?" I asked. That hurt him, but he respected my question and overlooked my ignorance.

"Never," he said with a pained look. "That would bring very bad luck."

On the way back to Pond Inlet, billows of fog rolled out of the snow-covered hills, limiting visibility to a doughnut hole of a hundred yards around our bumping komatics. The guides were eager to get home, and I was hoping to make it in time for Pond Inlet's high-school graduation, an event our bed-and-breakfast hosts had invited us to attend. We made one quick stop to retrieve cached fuel, and another for lunch.

With the snowmobiles quieted at the lunch stop, the nearby fog-covered hills became alive with sound. Four noisy snow geese winged over us, but there were more sounds—sounds I had heard before but could not place.

"Sandhill cranes," Dave said. "This is the northern limit of their breeding grounds."

I noticed Mathias putting his rifle in his snowmobile scabbard and filling a pocket with ammunition.

"Going hunting?" I asked.

"Yup." Mathias said, and Dave nodded his approval. You cannot expect a lifelong hunter to forgo all opportunities for a guiding job. They had to eat, and I was glad to see him pursuing country food low in POPs.

"May I join you?"

"Yup."

I grabbed my camcorder, jumped behind him, and we were off through the fog.

I had to hang on for dear life as Mathias negotiated the stacked ice of pressure ridges on his way toward shore. Near shore, he stopped to point out a gyrfalcon. We went up a valley filled with deep, wet snow. Mathias had all he could do to control the snowmobile and keep it upright as we gained altitude through the slush. I saw a pair of snow geese on open tundra and tapped him on the back. Two shots from his small-bore rifle guaranteed two geese for his family's dinner. Within twenty minutes, he had bagged eight.

I arrived at the high-school gymnasium just in time for the graduation ceremony. Most of the 1,300 residents showed up for the festivity. A traditional seal-oil lamp-lighting by an elderly lady and drum dancing by a young man opened the ceremony. The class valedictorian gave a speech in Inuktitut and English. Inuktitut from a beaming young lady was surprisingly melodic compared to the camp discussions of Mathias and Leuty. The valedictorian was a special lady of twenty-five, with two children and a proud, tuxedoed husband.

I took a late morning walk around the hills of Pond Inlet and remembered shopping at the co-op store the previous summer. In August, their offerings of local arts and handicrafts were picked over by an increasing number of tour-boat crowds. Now, the selection was outstanding, and I focused on beluga and narwhals carved from caribou antlers. Mounted on a tripod of antler, they looked graceful and alive. Individual carvings behind the locked glass cage were priced at about a hundred dollars. I reached for my wallet and turned to look for a clerk.

Instantly a short, animated Inuk was at my side. "What are you looking for?" he said, taking my elbow and leading me back to the display. "What do you like?"

"I like the caribou-antler whales."

"Beluga or narwhal?"

"Both."

"On the same mount?"

"That would be nice," I said, feeling like I was in a Tijuana flea market.

"Don't pay those prices," he said—and I expected to hear "Señor," but it was, "Don't pay those prices, Mel. Not for that junk."

Was he reading my Visa card through my wallet? How did this stranger know me? I looked into the grinning face of Silas, a hunter I'd met, along with his twelve-year-old son Jeremiah, on the edge. I'd only seen him in sealskin pants and fur parka and didn't recognize him in jeans and a flannel shirt.

"Silas!" I exclaimed. "Great to see you."

"Me too," he said hurriedly. "You want a beluga and a narwhal on a mount?"

"I'd love it," I said, "but there's none here."

"I'll get you one."

"Where?"

"Make it," he said, with a confident, toothy grin.

"I'm leaving early in the morning," I said, thinking he couldn't possibly work that fast.

"No problem."

"How much?

"A hundred bucks."

"OK."

"You at the Cedar Inn?"

"Yes."

"See you at seven."

I wondered what I had gotten myself into. In less time than I could split a small pile of firewood, he was going to create art? I didn't think so.

Silas came to the Cedar Inn as we were wrapping up with Leuty and Dave after dinner. Mathias had taken his pay and left for a hunting trip. I met Silas at the door, and he offered a cloth-wrapped bundle that I carefully unwrapped to reveal an exquisite rendering of intertwined and balanced whales on a single mount. They looked playful and free, a perfect rendering of life at the ice edge. I was elated and brought Silas into the dining room to share it. Another guest, an artist from Toronto who was staying for a few more days, ordered a larger version, and the others ordered carvings to be shipped.

I did not learn much about POPs on this trip, and what I did learn was disturbing. The Inuit and their education system knew nothing of the harm of POPs. In their minds, the contamination discovered fifteen years ago in Broughton Island had been cleaned up. According to any information they received, consumption of country foods was a healthy choice.

Getting to know a few Inuit was far more valuable than attaining a slight increase in my scientific understanding of the source, transport, fate, and effect of toxic, persistent, bioaccumulative pollutants. POPs contamination of the north would never again be the problem of a remote band of aboriginals. Inuit were now personalized by Leuty, Mathias, Silas, Jeremiah, a baby crying softly from a komatic visiting at our camp in the early morning, and a proud high-school valedictorian with her husband and children.

I had made arrangements to meet with the nurse and hamlet officials in Broughton Island on my return south. They would certainly have a feel for historical contamination, and sensitivity to the levels of POPs in country foods.

The commercial flight from Pond Inlet to Iqaluit lacked the intimacy with the coastal landscape I had enjoyed in Paddy's Twin Otter. Our direct route to Clyde River took us high over Baffin Island's snow- and glacier-covered mountains. When we did glimpse the shoreline, its fjords and bays were iced over well into the iceberg-spotted open waters of Davis Strait.

On the approach to Clyde River, the surrounding hilltops poked through thick fog rivers drifting down from glacier-covered mountains. The Hawker-Sidley dropped down for a look, saw no breaks in the cover, accelerated back to flying altitude, and set a course toward Broughton Island. The pilot announced he would be "over-flying" Clyde River, evidently a common occurrence.

At Broughton Island, an onshore breeze had lifted the fog, allowing an approach over the ice-covered ocean. The town of 500 lay close to the ice, with prefabricated houses and civic buildings mounted on permafrost protecting poles, or sprawled over outcropping rock.

While the luggage was offloaded, my ice-edge trip mates and Jacques, the cook who was traveling to another assignment, bid me goodbye from the airport's muddy apron. Their eyes reflected my fears. Would I ever get out of here? The wind-raised ceiling was at a barely acceptable level, and the crew was eager to get airborne. If my outbound trip out was "over-flown," I could end up here for another week! The Clyde River Inuit did not appear to worry about landing in the wrong hamlet and were warmly greeted by Broughton Islanders, friends or relatives eager to be caught up on their winter's news.

I ducked into the terminal, a two-room wooden shack, to see if Broughton Island's public buildings advertised the benefits of country food. A glossy poster proclaimed the spiritual, cultural, and health benefits of country food and encouraged consumption without reservation or concern. The AMAP study had recommended educating Inuit regarding the POPs in their foods in order to make intelligent and informed choices. The study from a decade ago showed that Broughton Island women of childbearing age were getting fifteen times the TDI of POPs, plus a dangerous load of mercury. Yet the government health agencies were proclaiming the values of toxic foods. Was I missing something?

I had arranged to be met by the hamlet's economic officer, given a tour of the town, and to meet with the Settlement Administrative Officer (SAO) and a hamlet nurse. It was not difficult to find my ride; there was only one vehicle outside the airport gate—a small, battered jeep accompanied by Tia, a tall Anglo with a welcoming smile.

"Welcome to Qikiqtarjuaq" *(Kee-kick-TAR-yachk)*, she said, using the Inuktitut name for the hamlet. "Where are you staying?" she continued, while clearing hunting and fishing equipment from one side of the jeep's cargo space to stow my luggage.

"The hotel," I said thinking that, as in Pond Inlet, a hotel or a bed-and-breakfast would be the choices.

"Which one?"

I fumbled for my reservations, finding none and surprised to hear that Broughton Island offered a choice of hotels.

"Don't worry," she said. "We'll stop at the hotel owner's house."

The manager was sleeping—must have been keeping Inuit hours, as it was nearly noon on a Friday. We drove past his hotel and confirmed, to my relief, that the "old" hotel was closed for the season.

"You must be at the Co-op Hotel," she said.

The Northern Co-op Hotel, sitting astride a line of rock jutting into the ice-covered bay, looked modern and inviting, but it was locked.

"We'll check at the store," Tia said. She informed me that there were two general stores and two hotels in the progressive town of Broughton Island. I was impressed, but dismayed to find the Northern Co-op Store also locked.

Tia drove to her office. "Blow the horn three times if you see anyone open the store," she said. "I'll call around."

A van pulled up to the Co-op Store and a woman with keys exited. The jeep's horn retrieved my host. "Quite an introduction to our metropolis," Tia laughed.

The manager's wife greeted us at the store, explaining that her husband was "working in the back" and had locked the door for security. My luck continued as, despite their having no record of my impending arrival, they had room. They gave us keys, and Tia drove me to the hotel. My meal plan included breakfast, lunch, and dinner. The manager showed up with a deli sandwich and choice of sodas after I had unloaded my bags into room no. 14 (of twenty).

The manager pointed to a phone hanging on the kitchen wall. Below it, a list of numbers and names was scrawled on the wall. "Call Lucy when you want dinner," he said. "My number is there if you need anything at all."

Tia left me with a package of information I had requested on POPs studies, and directions to her house. "Come over about one," she said. "Leslie can take you onto the ice before you meet with Don." Leslie, Tia's husband, was a guide, and Don was the Settlement Administrative Officer, Broughton Island's city manager.

I unpacked and surveyed my newfound "ownership" of the Northern Co-op Hotel. The dining room had seating for forty, a small dance floor or stage, and a television. A wall of long and narrow windows would have afforded an excellent view of the bay if their multipane seals had not failed. They were opaque with internal moisture. I snooped around, finding the kitchen well stocked and the freezer filled with market food. The posted menu indicated steak for tonight's dinner.

Taking the best seat in the house, I turned on the TV news, unwrapped my sliced-turkey sandwich, popped a soda, and opened Tia's envelope. Tia's information was disappointing. I had hoped for an update of POPs studies that must have followed the local breast-milk scare in the mid-1980s. There were a few studies of PCBs and DDT in various birds and animals, but no human studies or updates of the dietary study.

The snowmobile tour of the ice with Leslie—a tall, stately elder whose bushy moustache hinted of Portuguese whaler ancestry—was exciting and informative. He carried a rifle and hoped to bag a baby seal for supper. We were unsuccessful and returned to his house for fruit and tea.

"How did the people of Broughton Island react to the PCB scare of the mid-1980s?" I asked, after we had engaged in a few moments of comfortable general conversation. "Do they worry about their food?"

"What was the PCB scare?" Tia asked. "I'd like to help, but I'm afraid I don't know what you're talking about."

I was shocked. Tia had come to Broughton Island on a teaching contract, married Leslie, and stayed on to help with Broughton Island's economic development. She and Leslie ran a guide service and a small gift shop. They were purchasing a tour boat to expand their guide business. How, in her years of working with the people of Broughton Island, could she not know of the chaos wrought when babies were taken from their mother's breasts and Broughton Island became known as "the contaminated island"?

I explained the breast-milk study in Canada's Great Lakes region, the scientists' desire for a pristine sample, and the shock at their findings in Broughton Island.

"I remember hearing about that on television," Leslie said. "They cleaned up the old weather station and the Dew Line base. There's no problem anymore."

I could have left it at that. Maybe I should have. The finding of gross contamination was explained away and solved by a superficial cleanup of nearby foreign military installations, and the natives were convinced their food was safe. They were happy with the situation, but could I leave them uninformed and happy?

Tia gave me an opening. "Do you feel there's still a problem?"

I summarized the dietary studies and AMAP's findings. I must have been convincing, because their attitude changed.

Tia looked at Leslie with a questioning raise of her eyebrows and touched her right hand to her left forearm.

"We've noticed seals with skin and organ disorders," Leslie said, looking out the window.

"And some hunters have itchy skin and sore spots," Tia said. "Leslie's worried about one on his arm. Could you take a look at it?"

"I'm an engineer, not a doctor," I said. "I've heard that mercury can give those symptoms, but I wouldn't recognize anything. What does your local nurse think?"

They both rolled their eyes and looked away at the suggestion of involving the nurse.

"It's time for your meeting with Don," Tia said, getting up to take me. They looked relieved to be finished talking about POPs and certainly did not want to involve the nurse.

I was eager to meet the city manager and find out how much he knew about POPs. So far, the disappearance of history was astounding, but should not have been surprising. Inuit are forward-looking, forgiving optimists who live in the present and leave the past forgotten. Anglos rotate through the area on two- to three-year contracts, leaving history behind as they rush home or to another contract.

I shuddered to think about the POPs load in nursing baby seals, but my testimony would be wasted on Leslie and Tia while their federal health agencies promoted country food. I was soon to learn more history and understand other benefits of baby-seal consumption.

THE HISTORY LESSON: JUNE 2001

Tia took me into the hamlet offices and down dark wooden corridors to meet Don, the SAO. The building interior reminded me of 1880s vintage mining-company offices in Michigan's Copper Country.

"Most of our furnishings were salvaged from the original Hudson's Bay Company installation," Tia said.

Don was in a corner office, humped over a gigantic wooden rolltop desk strewn with books, papers, and documents. His lap and the chairs on either side of his desk were covered with "work in progress." He appeared to be an intense and serious young man. Tia had told me he was from the western prairies, was married to a local Inuk, and had three small children.

"Excuse the mess," Don said, putting his pencil behind his ear and extending his hand. "Three proposals are due to Yellowknife by the end of next week. How can I help?"

"Mel's the environmental engineer with an interest in the PCB crisis of 1985," Tia said. "I've supplied him with some recent studies, but he wondered if you have any historical records."

"Oh yes," Don said, recalling a forgotten conversation with Tia. Obviously, my visit didn't have the priority of his proposals to the territorial government. "You're welcome to anything we have—they're public records," he continued, and pointed down the hall.

I thanked him and left with Tia down hallway floors of time-stained maple. The dark oak door frames, high wooden wainscoting, and thick frosted glass soaked up most of the light coming from the occasional bare incandescent bulb dangling from the ceiling. The file room was the dead-end section of a remote hallway. Filing cabinets opened from each side into the narrow hall.

This was not Tia's home turf, and she struggled with the filing system in the dim light. We opened and closed a few musty drawers, getting a feel for how things were filed.

"What was the PCB crisis?" Don said from behind us.

"Southern researchers found high concentrations of PCBs in the milk of your women in 1985," I said. "It created quite a stir."

"Never heard of it," Don said. "But that doesn't mean we don't have records. I've only been here four years, and there have been at least three Settlement Administrative Officers since '85. Let's see what we can find."

Don located the mid- to late-1980s records and rifled through a foot-thick area of documents.

"This may be of interest," he said, handing me a faded blue folder. There were copies of papers and abstracts bound together with a white plastic spine.

The label pasted on the cover identified it as the "Studies of the Distribution of Chlorinated Hydrocarbon Pesticides and PCBs in the Arctic Ocean, 1986–1988."

"It could be," I said, struggling to read it in the darkness.

"I'll get you better light," Don said. "Coffee?"

"Please," I said, glad to see him developing an interest.

"Take a good look," Don said, setting me up at a hallway table directly under a dangling incandescent bulb. Tia returned with coffee and excused herself to catch up on office work. Don turned to leave.

I hurriedly opened the collection of papers on the distribution of POPs in the Arctic Ocean. In spite of indoor temperatures that allowed you to see your breath, the musty aroma drove me into a sneezing spasm—a violent, noisy, and uncontrollable act I go into when stimulated by a dose of mold or pollen. What a time to make a scene, I thought.

Don stopped in his tracks. "You going to be all right?"

I nodded, struggling to control the sneezing, with my eyes tearing, hoping he would just leave me alone. He did.

Sitting under the circle of golden incandescent light, I pinched myself, not believing who or where I was. I was above the Arctic Circle, in a 1800s trading-outpost office with access to the records of one of the most mysterious environmental findings in history. Was this real? If not, I had better hurry before reality returned.

The papers described 1984 efforts to set up a research station on a two-and-a-half-by-four-mile ice island floating in the Arctic Ocean. In 1986–88, extensive POPs sampling took place during the summer months. The island was thirty miles from Ellesmere Island at the time of the samplings.

The collection of published papers, notes, conference proceedings, and papers submitted for publication was a treasure trove of knowledge regarding scientific understanding of the late 1980s. Hexachlorocyclohexane (HCH) was the most abundant POP, followed by hexachlorobenzene, toxaphene isomers, chlordane, PCBs, and DDT.

Concentrations in deep ocean water showed the less salty surface waters to have a higher concentration of POPs than the Atlantic Ocean to the south. The surface-water concentrations surrounding the ice island were higher than in freshwater rivers from Russia and North America. Researchers concluded that "atmospheric transport was the major source of organochlorines to the Arctic Basin." According to this 1986 report, the Arctic Ocean, just like Lake Superior, was receiving POPs from the air.

Samples of biota from the ice island quantified bioaccumulation of POPs through the food chain, finding 0.300 ppm (parts per million) of chlordane, 0.870 ppm of DDT, and 0.627 ppm of PCBs in ringed seals. In the summer's Arctic air, hexachlorocyclohexane was found at 500 picograms per cubic meter. I was wondering how many molecules per breath that amounted to when I realized Don was at my side.

"Interesting?" he asked as I looked up.

"Very," I said. "I didn't realize that so much was understood about Arctic Ocean contamination in the late 1980s, or that the scientists had already implicated air transport as their source."

"You might be interested in this," he said, handing me an inch-thick stack of double-spaced typed pages. "It's a transcript of something related to the contamination. I didn't find anything else of interest in the files."

I suddenly realized he had been searching files while I was reviewing the research papers. Why the sudden interest and support when he was busy with proposal deadlines?

"In your career, have you been involved in the assessment of contaminated sites?" Don asked.

"Many."

"Could you look over an assessment report for me?"

"I'd be happy to," I said, standing to join him.

"Give me an hour to clear up a proposal," he said. "If that report doesn't amuse you enough, feel free to search the files for more."

The transcript was of a 1989 hearing on "Consideration of the Matter of Arctic Contaminants." Government leaders—I assumed the territorial government in Yellowknife, Northwest Territories—was taking the testimony of scientists, and comments from concerned groups. It was comprehensive, nearly a hundred pages. Acids, metals, radioactivity, and POPs were discussed, with POPs getting most of the focus.

The director of resource planning and coordination for the Department of Indian Affairs and Northern Development talked about POPs, their banning in North America, and their continued transport to the Arctic. He mentioned the cleanup of twenty-one DEW Line (Distant Early Warning) cold-war radar sites, and how they were not a significant contributor to the current PCB contamination.

I found it amazing that it was known that the DEW Line bases were not a significant POPs source in 1989, yet papers Tia provided to me described recent government-funded research to study birds nesting near Broughton Island to determine if local sources of PCBs were influencing them and the local population eating them. In another effort, a local senator established a charity dedicated to removing the PCBs from drinking water to protect his voters. You could drink water until you drowned before getting the amount of PCBs in one serving of narwhal muktuk! How could the government and its scientists understand that PCB contamination is sourced from long distances and concentrates up the food chain, and then waste resources and add to confusion by addressing local and meaningless issues? The results of mixing science and politics are truly amazing. Back to the hearing transcript.

The speaker stated that POPs were rather uniformly distributed across the Arctic. He did not know how they got there, but was confident they came from the Northern Hemisphere—probably the United States. He explained that arctic char had about one-tenth the toxaphene contamination levels as trout from the Great Lakes, and beluga in the St. Lawrence contained twenty-five times the PCBs as Arctic beluga. Bioaccumulation up the food chain was explained and frustration expressed about trends over time. Over the previous decade, PCBs and DDT were decreasing in seals, but polar bears had four times the chlordane and twice the PCBs. He introduced the next speaker by saying that the benefits of nutrition had to be balanced with the risk of contaminants in the diet.

The testimony continued with a doctor from Health and Welfare Canada who explained how the benefits of nutritious country food and breast-feeding outweighed any health concern, how PCB analysis was "fraught with uncertainty," and that calculation of Tolerable Daily Intake (TDI) of PCBs contained factors of safety. What a whitewash, I thought as I read the testimony. He only addressed PCBs, the POP contributing less than 10 percent of the TDI of all POPs combined in the study he referred to during his talk. He said nothing about mercury or the POPs pesticides.

A professor of nutrition testified that all foods, including southern market foods, contain PCBs. Her message was that country food contained protein, healthful fats, vitamin A, iron, and zinc—nutrients that protected the heart and immune system, fought cancer, prevented anemia, and kept the inhabitants from going blind. Switching from country food to market food would cause diabetes and other diseases. She carefully referred to market food as "bought," assuming that Inuit would only be able to afford low-nutrient starches, sugars, and junk food to replace their country food. She finished with a plug for breast-feeding and, like the previous speaker, never mentioned mercury or any POP other than PCBs.

The president of the Dene Nation and Métis Association, an Indian or "First Nations" organization, offered eloquent testimony, bringing the officials to task for pointing out problems of contamination above standards and then saying the standard was meaningless. His aboriginal people expressed the need for access to information, their own experts, and meaningful participation in the process. He urged the support of an international effort to stop the pollution of his once pristine land, and demanded full participation of aboriginal representatives in all aspects of the process.

The Broughton Island mayor's concerns were read by a representative of the Inuit Circumpolar Conference (ICC), an international organization representing Inuit of Alaska, Greenland, and Canada. The mayor was concerned that the same experts who had been filling the newspapers with stories of serious concerns about the contamination two and a half months earlier were now saying that there was no problem. Who should his people believe? The mayor requested timely information to quell the apprehension felt in his community. This hearing was held in late winter of 1989, and he felt the plan to bring experts to Broughton Island for an information meeting in May was too late. I had found no evidence that information was ever received.

The ICC representative then continued with her own comments. She thanked the scientists for recommending that Inuit continue to eat their food, and explained her organization's dedication to work internationally to find and control the long-term sources of POPs. She emphasized the necessity of full participation of aboriginal organizations, and the need for effective, timely, and sensitive communication of risks and benefits.

I sat back and reflected on the testimony, in the cold of my unheated hallway office. The hearing must have followed the release of the dietary study comparing POPs ingested by the terrestrial Dene/Métis and the Broughton Island women who consumed marine mammals. This study was a follow-up to the earlier sampling of PCBs in human milk at Broughton Island.

The comprehensive dietary study showed that Broughton Island Inuit were ingesting many times the TDI of several POPs, with chlordane and toxaphene being of greatest concern; but the medical and health experts focused only on PCBs. The PCB level was near the TDI, and of little real concern compared to the outstanding nutritional value of country food. In their damage-control efforts, the politicians dodged the toxicity of the POPs pesticides and mercury while comparing the benefits of country food to only the risks of PCBs. The aboriginals were asking for risk-and-benefit comparisons to make their own decisions, and the risks were being blatantly ignored.

It was amazing that a dozen years later, the general feeling in the Arctic was that PCBs were the problem, military installations were the source, and the food was now safe. Every person I had talked to in the Arctic, including educators, airline executives, and hamlet officials, was convinced that problems with contaminated food were issues of the past. With constant government communication on the benefit and safety of country food, it was no wonder.

I had considerable sympathy with the Broughton Island mayor's concern about "flip-flopping" experts. I had read an article by a researcher who was initially concerned about the effects of PCBs and was now suddenly praising the omega acids in PCB-laden muktuk. Did his research funding depend upon following the government's line?

The aboriginal requests for inclusion in the process of international efforts to find and stop sources of POPs seemed to have gone forward. Aboriginals were key players in negotiations with the United Nations Environmental Programme (UNEP) efforts to globally ban POPs, and had obtained funding for aboriginal input into the Arctic Monitoring and Assessment Programme.

I was asking myself why the Canadian government would warn their southern population of the dangers of mercury, PCBs, and POPs pesticides, while encouraging Inuit to freely consume food with toxic levels in excess of all standards, when Don returned.

"Do you have time for a tour?" he asked.

"Certainly," I said, eager to forget about the incongruous governmental actions and see some daylight. I would get the daylight, but was in for another dose of politics from Broughton Island's SAO.

THE SAO

"Let's take a look at a couple of reports on the way out," Don said, directing me into his office. It had been cleaned up considerably, and three familiar-looking colorful binders were displayed on his table.

"Your environmental studies?" I asked, recognizing the standard binding and format used by environmental consultants.

"On PCBs at the old Dew Line installation up the hill," Don said. "The Military College came up last year to do the assessment and wants to return to perform the cleanup this summer. I have to sign off on their plan to get them to return." He spoke calmly, but appeared to have trouble controlling outrage.

"Problems?' I asked.

"There's a lot of this I don't understand," he said. "But I'm concerned that they're locking me out of the work and might contaminate our water supply with their solution. Can you help me through the technical stuff?"

"Sure," I said, thumbing my way through the all-too-familiar standard assessments while Don went on to explain how he was locked out of the project.

The site had been cleared of PCBs years ago, but there was federal money available to assess and address any potential for residual contaminants, and it would be spent. The Military College environmental-assessment crew was made up of French-speaking Canadians from Quebec. They set up a camp outside of town and employed the minimum federal requirement of local labor: a polar-bear watch and a janitor. The Municipality of Broughton Island received a small fee for water supply and sewage removal.

"You didn't get a lot of help with your unemployment," I said, realizing that Broughton Island's unemployment was more than 35 percent and Don's main job was supplying employment opportunities.

"Two lousy jobs and an undesired contribution to the diversity of our gene pool is all Broughton Island got out of last summer's effort," Don muttered.

The plan was to return with equipment and operators to physically remove residual construction debris and landscape the area in a manner that would prevent Inuit contact with any residual PCB-contaminated soil. Any construction material of value had been removed by locals years ago. A quick look through the assessment report showed the remaining soils to be far less contaminated than much of the country food they were told to eat.

"You have trucks and drivers," I said. "Why can't you do the cleanup?"

"We'd have to be trained in hazardous-waste handling," Don said. "But that's a small problem. I can't even bid on the project."

"Why not?" I asked. "You've obviously got good people here; your streets are the best I've seen in the Arctic."

I couldn't have said anything better to gain Don's friendship. I'd recognized his pride in his town and the skill of his people. His tenseness gave way to a warm smile.

"I can't bid because only Inuit organizations can bid," he said, shaking his head.

"That's incredible," I said. "At 95 percent Inuit, you're the most Inuit hamlet in the Arctic."

"But not an Inuit organization," he said. "Bidding is reserved for Inuit-controlled, incorporated entities."

"So the work is done by imported labor from Quebec instead of local Inuit."

"Exactly. And if I don't approve their plan, they threaten to set up their own camp, with water supply and sewage treatment of their own."

"These studies look like they were designed for southern Quebec," I said. "They planted monitoring wells and expected to find groundwater. Did they know they would encounter permafrost?"

"You catch on fast," Don said and reached for his jacket. "They were clueless."

Don's pride in his hamlet and people became more apparent as we toured the town from his pickup. He'd developed a clam-harvesting business supplying Canada's western provinces with fresh clams. This required training Inuit in dry-suit diving, through the ice in the winter and from boats in the summer. As a survivor of one week of dry-suit diving on wrecks in Lake Superior's Isle Royale area, I was impressed. Teaching safe and effective diving in Inuktitut would be a considerable challenge. Don explained how he had planned and executed the training and achieved 100 percent graduation with no accidents.

Don also explained how the global backlash against fur garments had dried up Inuit jobs in seal-fur trading. Seals were still harvested for food, and the locally made fur garments were works of art, but there was very little employment generated. There was a developing market for seal-leather gloves and handbags, and they hoped to develop a handicraft business based on locally tanned leather. As we drove past the wastewater treatment area, I cautioned Don concerning the toxicity and persistence of most tanning chemicals. He assured me that they were pursuing an environmentally friendly solution.

Don's concerns about the proposed PCB cleanup were that the operation would raise dust and pollute his drinking-water supply. We could not visit the site, because the road was blocked in places with snow, and the lower stretches were too bare to snowmobile. I had enough of an orientation to understand the reports without seeing the site.

Don took me back to his office to retrieve the environmental reports and the material I had found in the files. He surprised me with another report he took from the top of his desk.

"I got this report a while back and really don't have the time or background to understand it," he said, handing me a copy of "Assessment of Dietary Benefit/Risk in Inuit Communities: August 2000." It was from the Center for Indigenous Peoples' Nutrition and Environment (CINE) of McGill University. "Could you look it over for me?"

"Gladly," I said, thumbing through the pages. It looked like an update to the study done to compare Broughton Island Inuit women with Dene/Métis aboriginal women consuming a terrestrial diet of country food—only this time, several Inuit coastal communities were compared. It would be interesting to see if Broughton Island's consumption of POPs TDIs increased with the government's marketing of the benefits of country food while downplaying the risks, and how Broughton Island compared to other communities. If the Arctic was really uniformly contaminated, POPs intake should be related to what Inuit ate, not where they lived. This study would be of real interest to me.

"Take it," he said, and began loading up the environmental reports. He dropped me off at the hotel with two boxes of material to review, excused himself to attend to family obligations, and asked me to meet with him at 9:30 the next morning.

The hotel's brightly lit dining room provided an excellent office area. I spread my assignments over two tables and laughed at my new job as environmental staffer to Broughton Island's SAO.

I took a walk around town to clear my head and plan the night's work. On the way back to the hotel, a female toddler fell off of her tricycle in her front yard. She was crying and seemed incapable of getting back onto her trike. Like any grandfather, I picked her from the muddy ground, righted her trike, and tried to get her back onto the seat. She seemed incapable of standing or supporting herself. Her father bolted from the front porch, putting his jacket on as he approached me.

"She can't walk," he explained in halting English, taking the little girl tenderly into his arms and comforting her in Inuktitut.

I wondered about the pristine Arctic. Whenever I flew, the flights carried at least one, and usually multiple families transporting a physically or mentally handicapped member. Were there widespread birth disorders in the north, or was I inferring more than really existed because of my concerns about POPs? Maybe the nurse could shed some light on that tomorrow. Tonight, I needed dinner and to review Don's reports.

A call to Lucy produced an efficient cook with two preteens and a toddler in tow. The kids were shy, and probably intimidated by the giant white guy with wisps of thin gray hair. I got a few words and smiles out of them before Lucy delivered my steak, snow peas, and potatoes, then herded them back into the kitchen to let me eat and read in peace. She cleaned up the kitchen and left me with a slice of homemade cherry pie. I thanked her and waved goodbye to the shy, grinning children hanging onto her coat. The food was tasty and quantities generous. I spread out the environmental reports and made ready to attack them, along with the pie and coffee. In the late evening Arctic twilight, large flakes of snow were visible through the fogged-up windows. I suddenly remembered that while I was on the ice edge, I had completely forgotten about the playoffs.

I turned on the TV to catch "Hockey Night in Canada" broadcasting the final Stanley Cup game. I had my own hotel, a hockey game, peaceful scenery, good food, and interesting reading. Could life be any better for a retired environmental engineer and ex–hockey coach?

The reports were typical assessments, covering all the required bases to describe the problem, determine the extent of contamination, propose alternatives, evaluate the risks and benefits, and recommend actions. I was through the site characterization and assessment by the end of the first period, and went to my room to retrieve a red pen for markups and comments. My door closed behind me and locked. I had left my keys on the dresser and was now locked out of my own room and confined to the public area of the hotel.

I checked the list of numbers at the wall phone, called the manager, and explained my dilemma.

"You watchin' the hockey game?" he asked.

"Ya eh," I answered in my best Canadian.

"I'll be there between periods," he said. "That guy who just scored for Colorado is a friend of my daughter's and I gotta see this."

He retrieved the keys in a touch-and-go between periods. By the end of the game I had assimilated the contents of the reports, understood their approach to a solution, and agreed with Don's concerns about excessive dust and dirt getting into his drinking-water supply. It had been a long day since leaving Pond Inlet. I slept like a log.

I woke up early, made a breakfast of instant coffee and rolls as hard as hockey pucks, and then opened the CINE updated nutrition report. One look at the report contents and I forgot about the lousy breakfast.

The updated results were dramatic and not good news for the Inuit. From the executive summary of the August 2000 report, the people of Broughton Island were ingesting 50 percent more chlordane, 100 percent more PCBs, and nearly three times more toxaphene than they did in 1987–88. The government's program to make certain the Inuit were not scared away from country food was working. They were consuming more, and the toxicity of the foods consumed had not decreased in the past decade.

Of the eighteen Arctic hamlets assessed, the mean consumption of chlordane and toxaphene was four times the TDI, and the 95th percentile group had ten times the TDI ingestion. This means that half the people were exposed to four times the TDI of toxaphene and chlordane, and one out of twenty was exposed to ten times the TDI. This exposure is excessive, well beyond the Lake Michigan sport-fish-eating mothers researched by the Jacobsens.

I was eager to get into the details of the report and see if these tremendous contamination loads were finally raising concerns in the health community. Unfortunately, the report still recommended unqualified consumption of country food. When would the government communicate the risks of POPs and at least encourage Inuit men and women of child-creating age to avoid the highly contaminated fat of marine mammals?

I was pretty worked up and in need of fresh air. I walked all through town, past the empty campground at its edge, and through the hills before bringing the box of environmental reports and papers to Don's office.

"Good morning," Don said, setting the box on a table. "Did you get through it? Any surprises?"

"No surprises other than the soils they worry about have lower PCB concentrations than muktuk does," I said, hoping to talk about food risks.

Don ignored the opening. "Do you see how they could dirty our potable water? Is there any reason I shouldn't be allowed to bid on the job?"

Don was focused on his response to the cleanup proposal, and getting his workers to do the job instead of putting up with another summer of imported southern laborers while Inuit remained unemployed. It was clear that he could not think about anything else, so we spent an hour and a half going through the technical details of the report and formulating a strategy for responding to Ottawa.

"I have to see Tia and get to a meeting with the nurse," I said, looking at my watch.

Don's eyes clouded with suspicion. "Why are you going to see her?" he asked.

"To find out what she knows about POPs and their effect."

"Do you have to?"

"She's the medical expert," I said, and Don's eyes now smoldered in hatred.

"She's useless," he said.

I interpreted his strong feelings as something deeply personal and not a professional judgment. I remained silent.

"For centuries, Inuit women have had their babies alone in birthing igloos," Don said in a barely audible monotone. "Now, in her thirty-fifth week of pregnancy, a woman must take what is very likely her first flight to go over the mountains and out of sight to a hospital in Iqaluit. Can you imagine the trauma?"

I nodded, thinking of some of the pregnant teenagers I'd seen getting onto a plane. Arctic air travel was an anxious experience for even the most seasoned of air travelers. It would be a terrible experience for a pregnant young wife or daughter to face.

"We've developed a midwife program," Don said, "but to have a baby anywhere other than the Iqaluit hospital requires permission of the nurse. Matilda won't give it."

"Why not?" I asked.

"Says we're all anemic."

"So take iron," I said, but wondered why their country-food diet didn't supply an abundance of iron.

"We do—but she says we don't and still calls us anemic. We defied her order and had our last baby at home; now she won't even talk to us. You still want to see her?"

"I do," I said, and made a mental note to check the iron intake of Inuit women in the nutritional part of the benefit/risk report.

"Can we meet this evening?" Don asked. "I'd like to be sure of this strategy."

"OK," I said, "I'll write up some conclusions for you. I'll also summarize the toxics data in the nutritional report. Some of the stuff looks scary."

"Not as scary as our nurse," Don said, forcing a weak smile. "Good luck with her."

THE NURSE

I met the nurse, Matilda, coming off her shift at the health center and crossing the road to her apartment. She was nearly six-foot tall. Penetrating light blue eyes and a freckled face surrounded by strawberry blond hair protruded out from her partially lowered snowmobile-suit hood. She gave me a pleasant smile and a firm, gloved handshake as we introduced ourselves.

"I'm ready for some tea and a visit, if you are," she said, inviting me into her apartment. She had a lilting Australian accent and pleasant demeanor. She did not seem to be the same person Don referred to with smoke in his eyes. Her apartment was neat and well appointed, but it was apparent she was packing household contents into boxes in the dining room.

"Are you leaving Broughton Island?" I asked.

"In five days, twenty hours, and sixteen minutes," she said, looking at her watch. "If by some miracle the plane is on time for once."

"Were you here for three years?" I asked, having heard that the Nunavut paid Australian nurses large bonuses if they contracted for a three-year tour. They were known to be well trained and independent.

"I got in on the two-year option," she said. "Good thing—I'd not be able to take another year here."

"Has it been that bad?"

"I enjoy being the chief medical officer and having a variety of work," she said, "but the people leave a lot to be desired."

"I've always found Arctic people pleasant," I said, "but then I'm a tourist."

"An ungrateful lot," she said. "They make you do your own work, from shoveling snow to fixing a snowmobile. You prescribe medicine for them and they don't buy it, and if you give it to them they don't use it. I'll be glad to go."

And they'll be glad when you're gone, I thought. How did this pleasant-seeming nurse and the accommodating Inuit ever get into such a state of misunderstanding and distrust?

"What was it you wanted?" she asked.

"I wondered what the chief medical officer of Broughton Island knew about the POPs contamination in country food, and what you thought about it," I said.

"POPs? What are they?" she said, to my surprise.

"PCBs and pesticides, such as DDT, toxaphene, and chlordane, that have made their way into the marine food chain," I said.

"I've just seen the signs around telling of the nutritional value of country food and how the Inuit shouldn't be concerned about the contamination," she said. "Do you see it a problem?"

"Here's a study of the dietary intake of aboriginal women," I said, handing her a copy of the comparative study. "It compares the POPs intake of Baffin Inuit with Arctic Indians."

"The Baffin girls are getting quite a load," Matilda said, taking the paper for closer examination. "I've never seen the likes of this before."

"This was prepared from data in the study," I said, showing her the table that added up the TDIs. "Would you recommend that people consume food containing fourteen times the Tolerable Daily Intake of pesticides and PCBs?"

"Good god no!" Matilda said, turning pale. "I was never told of any problem levels of toxics in country food." She was visibly shaken. "Wait a minute," she added. "North America banned these things. The food should be cleaner now. It must be, because Ottawa's pushing country-food consumption."

I showed her the new report I'd gotten from Don. "This is the latest data from the Center for Indigenous Nutrition and Environment," I said. "Broughton Island's status can be compared to the report of ten years ago. Currently the rate of ingestion of chlordane is 50 percent higher, PCBs have doubled, and toxaphene nearly tripled."

"It's worse than it was ten years ago," Matilda said, barely above a whisper. "Is Broughton Island unique because of ocean currents and military bases?" This was a common logic I'd heard people use to explain the contamination of Broughton Island and assume a lack of contamination in other communities.

"No," I said, opening the report to a page comparing contaminants in various hamlets. "The ingestion level depends on diet. People from remote island communities are more dependent on marine mammals for food, and therefore the most susceptible to high levels of contamination."

"They get any mercury?" Matilda asked. "I've seen it in Australia."

"The Nunavut-wide average mercury ingestion is near the Tolerable Daily Intake," I said, turning to another page. "But in the remote communities, a quarter of the people ingest four times the TDI, and 5 percent get nine times.

"What TDI are they using?" Matilda asked.

I rifled quickly through the report. "Point seven micrograms per kilogram per day," I said, pointing to the reference.

"Bloody generous," Matilda said. "For methyl mercury, the form present in seafood, I've seen TDIs less than half that level."

"Meaning?"

"It could be twice as bad," Matilda said. "Could explain some of their depression and irrational, violent behaviors."

"There was a study sponsored by eight polar nations," I said, taking out the AMAP summary report. "The last chapter addresses potential human problems from POPs and mercury ingestion by Inuit in the Canadian Arctic and Greenland."

"Why did they focus on this part of the Arctic?" Matilda said, standing up to stretch, holding the report.

"Because of the presence of isolated populations that depend on marine mammals, the source of highest concentrations of POPs," I said. "Take a look at this list of human effects. Have you seen any?"

Matilda read for a moment. The color left her face as she gasped, her hand coming to her throat.

"What's wrong?" I asked.

"They mention immune-system suppression, and I've seen kids with constant infections, so bad and for so long that the tykes suffered permanent hearing loss. Excessive mercury could be causing their anemia, because mercury replaces iron in the blood. Mercury also causes skin irritations, and this is widespread in elders. Women bring me their husbands who are having tremors, something I thought came from drinking wood alcohol, but it could be the mercury. POPs and mercury can cause fetal disorders ranging from death to physical and mental impairments or learning disorders."

"Have you seen birth defects?" I asked.

"I've certainly seen a higher proportion of handicapped children in the Arctic than I've noticed anywhere else," Matilda said. "But that's anecdotal, not scientific data. We tend to blame fetal alcohol syndrome, but I've seen too many in utero fetal deaths in the little time I was here, and none of the women were drinkers."

Matilda sat in silence for a moment, "The Center for Indigenous Peoples' Nutrition and Environment study must contain nutrient data," she said, leafing through the report and stopping to carefully study a page. "Unbelievable," she said, setting the report on the counter.

"What?" I asked.

"Broughton Islanders are getting twice the minimum daily requirement of iron in their diet, but they're anemic," Matilda said.

"Why?" I asked.

"I'd strongly suspect mercury; it replaces the iron in hemoglobin, making it useless for transferring oxygen," Matilda said, and then muttered, "No wonder they run out of energy."

I paced about the apartment, collecting my thoughts. Matilda also appeared to be contemplating and sorting the new information.

"And I accused them of not taking their iron pills," she said softly as she sat on the couch.

I admired a half-packed soapstone eagle on the dining-room table and picked it up for a closer look. It stood on a jagged stone perch, with every feather of its nine-inch wingspan finely carved into the jade-and-gold variegated stone. The head and talons were detailed in ivory. Its rugged beauty was captivating.

"I've been wondering how to box that," Matilda said. "Be a shame for him to arrive home in pieces."

"Is this from Broughton Island?" I asked. "Can I get one?"

"Tony O, a local carver, made it," Matilda said. "'Took a nasty fall chasing narwhal in his boat. Busted up his wrist pretty bad and thought he'd never carve again. This was the first thing he carved after his recovery, and he gave it to me—just walked into the clinic one day, handed it to me, turned around, and left."

"Would he make one for me?" I said.

"Oh no," Matilda said. "He'd never do the same thing twice."

I managed to talk Matilda into selling it to me if I promised to carry it carefully home in my backpack. It remains a treasured reminder of the trip and Matilda's realization of her misjudging of the Broughton Island Inuit. I hope it guards me from judging before understanding.

"I've got to run to a meeting with the Girl Scouts," Matilda said while pulling up her boots. "Thanks for the chemistry lesson. Wish I'd have gotten it on my arrival instead of my departure. Lock the door on your way out."

I shook my head to clear my thinking as I put on my boots and coat in the anteroom. Why would Matilda not have had access to POPs information? It certainly would have helped her do her job, and perhaps even changed her attitude. I gathered up my papers and the carving and returned to the hotel to finish the work for Don.

BROUGHTON ISLAND WRAP-UP: JUNE 2001

I used my private hotel dining-room office to spread out and organize the environmental studies. Don was very interested in my input, and I had promised him a summary report. I didn't sense the same degree of interest in the Center for Indigenous Peoples' Nutrition and Environment (CINE) report, and wanted to develop a presentation in a way he could understand and hopefully respond to the gross contamination of country food. I quickly finished the environmental summary, packed up the report binders, and concentrated on the CINE report.

The CINE study was developed in 1997–98, data collected in 1998–99, and the report issued in 2000. The study's objectives were to derive quantitative estimates of country and market food use in representative communities; complete the database on nutrient and contaminants in food; define the nutritional, socioeconomic, and cultural benefits of country food; and define the level of contaminants in Inuit diets.

After a quick read of the report, I feared that the study design and interpretation were slanted heavily toward the benefits of country food, with the risks being downplayed or ignored. The nutritional scientists had legitimate concern about the Inuit's trend to eat less country food. There was an alarming rate of obesity among North Americans in general, and aboriginals in particular, as diets changed from meat and natural fats to sugar and processed fats. Purchase of market food high in saturated fat and sugars resulted in a nutritionally poorer diet than the country food obtained by hunting and gathering. In addition to superior nutrition, country food supplied exercise, economic benefits, and cultural and spiritual experiences. When Inuit were surveyed concerning their preference for country food, without any mention of the POPs or mercury content and the associated risks, they had a strong preference for country food.

I thought back to the hearing record of a decade ago. The request of the Dene/Métis president was ignored. He wanted aboriginal people to have access to all the data and to make their own choices. This study did not give Inuit data on the presence of POPs in the various foods they consumed, the Tolerable Daily Intake of these foods, and the risks of exceeding the TDIs. The scientists collected and reported the data in a way that made up the Inuit's minds for them, assuming that they would put a high value on the cultural, economic, and spiritual content of the food and ignore any possibilities of birth defects, anemia, compromised immune systems, and infertility.

In a section titled "Findings in Perspective," the report stated that because of a lack of time to prepare country food due to work, school, or child care; the lack of expensive equipment to harvest country food; or weather changes, many Inuit were consuming less country food than they did five years before. Quoting the report, "Strategies to improve the use of available and culturally acceptable traditional food to improve nutrient intake and health need to be proactive, and in careful consideration of other factors influencing food choices, such as the fear of contaminant risks."

My blood boiled and I saw red! Inuit were not told about contamination because they would be scared away from country food. I slammed the report onto the table and paced the dining room, unable to sit. Why not at least tell the men and women of child-creating age about the risks, the contaminant levels in country foods, and let them make their own choices? Terrestrial Inuit and northern Indians consume country food and do not ingest a dangerous level of POPs or mercury. By avoiding the fats of mammals high on the marine food chain, Inuit could drastically cut their POPs intake and still have a nutritious diet. How could a governmental health agency tell someone to consume poison because it is good for them? I needed some fresh air and to put my own findings into perspective.

The CINE report, and previous reports, had identified the need for education to allow informed choices, but there was no communication beyond stating that country food is good, market food is bad . . . eat country food. The nurse wasn't even made aware of POPs, and the report sent to the town government wouldn't have been read if Don hadn't given it to me. The principal of Pond Inlet's school thought POPs contamination was an isolated incident of Broughton Island's past, something local to Broughton Island because of its DEW Line base and ocean currents. Nobody in the Arctic was being given facts from which they could make informed choices.

Looking over Broughton Island's bays and toward the nearby mountains of Baffin Island, I could imagine the rugged fjords in the distance, the scene of last fall's narwhal hunt. One-hundred and thirty-five of these majestic beasts were captured and many more killed, when the federal government had historically limited the fall hunt to twenty-five. No wonder the latest CINE report had the Broughton Island residents eating more narwhal muktuk and greatly increasing their toxaphene and chlordane intake. There was an infinite supply. I'd have to ask Don about that hunt.

I wondered about the long-term supply of country food. The current Inuit are descendants of people who entered the Arctic a thousand years ago. They were creative nomads who had developed the use of dogs for transportation and successfully hunted the bowhead whale. These giants supplied food, oil for heat and light, and construction materials for sleds, tools, and shelters. Nomadic Inuit successfully displaced or assimilated all previous human Arctic inhabitants. Then, Europeans and Americans hunted their whales to near extinction and made them into city dwellers. Now, outsiders protest the occasional harvest of a single bowhead whale.

Without the bowhead, Inuit hunt beluga and narwhal, much smaller animals. Every community complains about its allotted quota of small whales—allotments determined by Ottawa scientists to assure a sustainable population. There are more Inuit in the Arctic than there were four hundred years ago, they are better equipped to hunt, and they have no access to their traditional major food supply, the bowhead. Will there be enough country food to continue to supply the growing Inuit population? If left to Inuit control, will the wildlife be decimated as it was in the fall narwhal hunt?

A walk on the bay certainly did not resolve my frustrations, but it was good to think about all the aspects of the Inuit diet in the context of history and their present social situation. I knew Don was unaware of the presence of dangerous levels of toxics in country food, and I wondered how he would accept the findings of the report. I wanted to make the report easy to understand, so I worked over some of the data.

Most importantly, the report showed that Broughton Island was not unique. Inuit ingested contaminants based on what they ate, not where they lived. Second, PCBs are a small part of the toxicity, and cleaning up the already cleaned-up DEW Line site will not make an iota of difference in toxicity to wildlife or humans. Third, the trend is not good. The twenty- to forty- year-old women of Broughton Island ingested 19 times the TDI of combined POPs instead of the 14.5 times found in the earlier study. Fourth, a small amount of highly contaminated foods is responsible for most of the POPs intake. A quarter-pound serving of narwhal blubber contains a half-year's TDI of POPs.

I had hoped to get Don to think about the toxics in various foods, make intelligent choices for his family, and hopefully educate others. The hotel menu called for pork chops for today's dinner, and a call to Lucy produced another excellent meal. I was finishing strawberry pie à la mode when Don arrived.

He asked about the environmental report, which I supplied to his satisfaction. I picked up the CINE report and sensed him backing away. He was not willing to hear about toxics.

"It looks like the fall of 1999's narwhal hunt provided a lot of food," I said as I looked at the report and dropped it into a box and out of his sight. It was time for lighter conversation. "Were you here for that?"

"My partner and I hunted it," Don said.

"What's a narwhal hunt like?"

"They cruise the shoreline, moving south for the winter," Don said. "We herd them into the fjords, where they're boxed in, and then circle them with our canoes."

"The big canoes?"

"A twenty-four footer with a 35-horsepower motor," Don said. "I was helmsman and Paulusi was up front with the rifle. When he shot one, I got him alongside so he could harpoon it to keep it from sinking."

"Was it orderly and organized?" I asked.

"It was chaos," Don said. "It's a wonder nobody got killed."

"How many did you get?"

"Three."

"Kill any that sunk?"

I got a cold "none of your business" look and silence. I assumed he had missed one or two and wouldn't talk about it.

"Could you use all the muktuk and meat?" I asked.

"We dragged them to shore and took the muktuk slabs, then left the meat to harvest later for dog food." Don said. "Every plane out took muktuk to surrounding towns, and we feasted on blubber and muktuk."

"A quarter-pound serving of narwhal blubber will give you all the toxics you can tolerate for half a year," I said, hoping to continue the discussion.

Don looked away and would not make eye contact. "Paulusi's a great hunting partner," he said, changing the topic. "He's also my best equipment operator, but he's unreliable."

I sat in silence, realizing toxics were not going to be a part of our conversation.

"He can't stay away from the land," Don continued. "I've had to fire him five times for absenteeism."

"But hire him back?"

"He's good—couldn't get along without him."

"Isn't it risky to be on the land with someone you just fired?"

"There's no hard feelings."

I thought it strange, but then everyone's needs were satisfied. Paulusi had the part-time job he wanted, and Don had a good worker and hunting partner.

"I even took Paulusi home with me to hunt the prairies," Don continued.

"Geese?" I asked.

"Yes," Don said. "My father nearly fainted when I ate the hearts and livers."

"Raw?"

"Fresh while cleaning them," Don said. "Best part of the goose."

"Do you eat the local game raw too?

"Muktuk of course, but fresh seal liver is out of this world," he said. "They really know how to eat up here."

I got the picture. Don had assimilated into the community and adopted Inuit culture. There was no way he would listen to concerns about toxics. He surprised me with his next statement.

"You know the real value of country food, don't you?" he said, pumping his fist in a sign of strength.

"Healthy hearts," I said, but wasn't grasping his message.

"Power," he said with a smile. "Real manpower."

"I get it," I laughed. "You really believe that?"

"It's real," he said, looking at me as though I had insulted his religion. "You should try a side of baby-seal ribs," he continued, coming alive. "They're fantastic! You really should try them."

I did not know if he wanted to send some home as a takeout order, or if he had local arrangements. I did not want to know, and changed the subject. We talked for another hour, avoiding toxics. I left in the morning, convinced that there was a need to communicate the risks of country food, and equally convinced it would be impossible to communicate something the government and its citizens did not want communicated. I needed to talk to the researchers who had been concerned about toxics and were now pushing country food.

FOLLOW-UP: AUGUST 2001

Back at home, a friend had sent me an interesting article from *Up Here*, a magazine from the Arctic. The article was entitled "Beluga and Seal Fat . . . It's Good for Your Heart," and pictured an Inuk cutting and eating a slice of raw muktuk. The point of the article was that these fats contained omega-3 fatty acids, a substance thought to prevent heart problems. A study of five hundred Inuit from northern Quebec found the incidence of heart disease to be half that of the rest of the people of Quebec.

A researcher I had recognized as one of the early leaders in concern about POPs in the environment was quoted as personally taking a daily fish-oil supplement and eating fish three times a week to gain the benefits of the Inuit diet. Why had he changed his mind and supported the consumption of seal and whale fat loaded with toxics? Of course, his personal consumption was fish-oil capsules and fish to get the omega-3 fatty-acid benefit without the high load of POPs.

I called and tactfully asked, "How in the name of all that's holy can you recommend the consumption of POPs-loaded beluga and seal fats? Weren't you warning about the harmful effects of POPs a few years ago?"

Being a gentleman, he did not hang up and calmly answered, "We've carefully considered the risk and health benefits of country food and recommend that our Quebec Inuit consume Arctic char, even when pregnant."

"Not a bad idea," I said, realizing the low levels of POPs in the tasty salmon-like fish. "But the article pictured a person eating raw beluga fat, and that contains hundreds of times the toxics levels found in char."

"We recommend that our Quebec Inuit consume char," he repeated.

"Do you tell them not to consume the fats from marine animals?"

"We recommend that our Quebec Inuit consume char, even when pregnant," he said.

"Thank you," I said, realizing I would get nowhere and concluding that his continued funding was probably contingent upon following some party line. Perhaps a CINE scientist could shed some light on the communication of toxic levels to Inuit.

I googled a coauthor of the CINE report and sent him an email expressing concern about the high concentration of POPs and mercury in the food he was recommending. He expressed his sharing of my concern and stated that he was working with local authorities to develop a method of communication and education that would not scare young people away from country food. I wanted to talk to him about minimizing the POPs intake of procreating Inuit, but he was leaving the country for a long vacation and conference. He agreed to meet me at the September 2001 IJC meeting in Montreal.

The attacks of September 11, 2001, caused the cancellation of the International Joint Commission (IJC) meeting. I phoned him and learned that in his judgment, the Inuit were much too ignorant . . . ah, er . . . uneducated to understand the levels of POPs in foods and make intelligent choices. But he was proud to announce that his research methodology was being recognized around the world, and he had requests from Alaska and other areas to conduct similar evaluations of aboriginal nutrition. For some reason, there was absolutely no interest in communicating the effects of toxics to Inuit.

I had thought that Canadian toxicity standards and Tolerable Daily Intake (TDI) recommendations were similar to U.S. standards, and could not imagine the Canadian government having dual standards of health protection. How would narwhal blubber compare to the latest Ontario fish advisory? I compared the narwhal blubber from the August 2000 CINE report to Ontario's 2001–02 fish advisory.

The narwhal blubber contained 4.8 ppm of PCBs. Ontario restricts fish with 0.5 ppm and recommends no consumption at 4.0 ppm. Toxaphene was at 44 times its restriction level, or 5.5 times its banning level of 1.6 ppm. The narwhal's chlordane content of 1.75 ppm is 5.8 times the U.S. FDA's action level.

This is a frightful dichotomy, and yet only part of the picture. Inuit mercury consumption is also far in excess of accepted health standards. The 29 May 2001 Canadian guideline for mercury consumption by women was one meal per month of fish containing 1.0 ppm mercury, which equates to about 10 percent of the TDI used in the CINE report. In Broughton Island, the average (mean) mercury consumption was twenty times the May 29 guideline, and 5 percent of the Broughton Islanders were over this guideline by a factor of a hundred and twelve. Nunavut's Inuit have mean mercury blood levels of 33.6 ppb, with a range of 1–225 ppb. The normally acceptable range is 20 ppb, with increased risk experienced at 20–100 ppb and risk a certainty at more than 100 ppb.

There is no scientific or humanistic logic to allow different standards for different humans. I remember how appalling it was to find that South American and African aboriginals were subjected to known and devastating mercury contamination in the mining of gold, and that radiation-exposure standards in African mines were much higher for blacks than whites. I hope common sense and the necessary hard work of communication will be instituted, and the poisoning of a great group of people stopped. Inuit have survived Western intrusions into their culture and food supply for six hundred years, and will understand and respond to the risk and benefit of the food we have poisoned if they are given the truth and a chance.

As I thought about differences in attitudes toward exposures to toxic chemicals, I reflected back to the 1991 IJC meeting, where concerns were expressed that anything above zero was intolerable, and banning of chlorine was recommended to save the Great Lakes ecosystem. The activists were adamant. Zero meant zero: not a single molecule. While reading the papers I had found describing 1980s research from an ice island in the Arctic Ocean, I wondered how many molecules of POPs were in a breath of Arctic air—or would it take several breaths to find a molecule?

I ran through some calculations on alpha-HCH, hexachlorocyclohexane. During the time of the ice-island study, large quantities of technical HCH were being used, and my calculations were indicating billions of molecules per breath.

In the Bermuda study, it was found that ocean air contained a constant amount of PCBs throughout a decade or more of measurement. I looked back at the study and found there were 76,000 molecules of PCBs per cubic centimeter, or two hundred million in a large breathful. In researching studies on PCBs in Michigan air, I found amounts equivalent to Bermuda levels in the summer, and much lower amounts in the winter.

Thoughts about consumption advisories caused me to wonder about toxaphene in Lake Superior. It was known to be present at five parts per million in trout, or twice the PCB concentration. Toxaphene is more toxic than PCBs having one-fifth its TDI, but in checking Michigan's fish-eating advisory, Lake Superior trout had restrictions because of their PCB content, but there was no mention of toxaphene.

I contacted the Michigan Department of Health to ask why Michigan had no toxaphene advisory. After several attempts, I was transferred to a "Dr. Something," who stuttered and stammered through an explanation of how the state used U.S. Food and Drug Administration guidelines. He could neither find nor refer me to the FDA guideline and suggested I contact them. In looking through the FDA website, I found lists of tolerances for all the POPs pesticides except toxaphene. An e-mail for help received a prompt reply from the FDA, stating that they used EPA-supplied tolerance levels. This was a surprise, because an EPA fact sheet[1] recommended no consumption of Lake Superior trout, warning that half a meal per month would supply toxaphene levels at the borderline of non-cancer problems and twenty-five times the cancer guideline.

Looking back, I found an older, 1993 revocation of the FDA's action levels for toxaphene. The agency, with few exceptions, had been unable to detect measurable levels of toxaphene in 40,000 food samples and stopped all toxaphene analysis on 30 September 1993. Michigan's fish-eating advisory, since they followed FDA guidelines, quit listing toxaphene restrictions. The 1999 EPA bulletin recommending no consumption of large Lake Superior trout did not trigger a revision in the FDA's guidelines or Michigan's advisories.

In 1996 and 1997, Michigan's Governor Engler pulled PCB advisories from the fish-eating guidelines and touted the lakes' cleanup to bolster tourism. He was severely criticized by the EPA, and PCBs reappeared in the 1998 advisories. Why didn't the EPA act on the whitewashing of toxaphene? Michigan and the United States have a different method of not communicating toxics information in a forthright manner, but it has the same results as that used by Canada and CINE. The public is uninformed and lacks information to make intelligent choices.

Enough politics. Let's get back to sorting out why the PCBs and toxaphene are staying in Lake Superior. The Arctic education may have helped.

---

1. EPA-823-F-99-018, September 1999.

TAKING STOCK: AUGUST 2001

Years of volunteer efforts, conferences, library research, and trips to the Arctic had left me with a massive amount of data on the source, transport, fate, and effect of POPs in the environment. As I mentally sorted the pile, some parts were enlightening, some confusing, and others conflicting. The Arctic Monitoring and Assessment Programme (AMAP) had done a great job of summarizing research results, and the August 2000 Center for Indigenous Peoples' Nutrition and Environment (CINE) report certainly documented the amount of POPs entering the Arctic food chain. But it was still not clear why the Great Lakes levels of PCBs, toxaphene, DDT, and chlordane were not disappearing, long after their banning. What was their continuing source?

In the years following the IJC's recommendation to ban chlorine, the USEPA, activist, and industrial focus on Pollution Prevention proved to be effective in reducing "toxics," those millions of tons of paint thinners, cleaning agents, and solvent emissions, but the hoped-for concurrent reduction in POPs did not materialize. I stifled the desire to say, "I told you so," as my environmentalist and regulatory friends slowly forgot about banning chlorine and gave up hope for Pollution Prevention as a POPs-reduction strategy.

Their new thrust was to clean up the Great Lakes' historical hot spots and "active sediments," those particles in the water column and the top 1.3 inches of the lake bottoms. They knew that these solids were now transferring contaminants to the water to maintain POPs concentrations at a nearly constant level.

According to the extensive Lake Michigan Mass Balance study, sediments contained 7,071 kilograms of PCBs, compared to only 690 kilograms in the water. Using EPA logic, the water column could not be cleaned up as long as these sediments were there to constantly supply PCBs to the water. If Congress could afford eight billon dollars to protect the Florida Everglades, couldn't they afford more than that to clean the Great Lakes sediments? I continued to doubt their logic. With Lake Superior's water and the air over it in equilibrium, removing sediments would not affect the concentration of PCBs in the water or its future sediments.

Finding that POPs moved toward the poles was certainly an unexpected revelation. Confirming this finding in Broughton Island's archives added to the believability of this unexpected long-distance transfer of chemicals of low volatility, but how were the POPs levels in Lake Superior being maintained? The little bit of toxaphene bleeding from cotton lands of decades past couldn't continue to support a concentration in Lake Superior and the Arctic. The United Nations Environmental Programme's POPs-reduction effort concluded that most of the POPs uses in the globe had been eliminated. Their priority was to clean up outdated stocks of chemicals sent to developing countries for mosquito and locust control by transferring them to developed countries with adequate destruction facilities.

My database was a logjam of complex and convoluted information on the source, transport, fate, and effect of POPs in the environment. A discussion with Uncle Reino led to better understanding of the fate of POPs in the environment and helped break that logjam.

POPS FATE: AUGUST 2001

Uncle Reino was eager to see my camcorder videos of the ice edge and hear of my research at Broughton Island. He was mesmerized by the close-ups of polar bears and narwhals, and then appalled by the amount of POPs the Inuit were ingesting.

"Sounds like a good trip," he said. "Are you figuring out where these chemicals are coming from?"

"I'm finding some interesting stuff, but it isn't coming together yet," I said.

"Do these POPs really go through the air all the way to the Arctic?" Reino asked.

"Remember what I told you about alpha-HCH being fifty times as concentrated in the Arctic Ocean as it was in oceans near its use points?" I asked Reino.

"That alpha-HCH was the major component of HCH used in foreign countries, wasn't it?" he replied.

"That's it," I said, wondering how many octogenarians would retain that tidbit for a year. "When the Asian countries learned how to make pure gamma-HCH, there was no more source of alpha-HCH."

"What happened to the concentration in the Arctic Ocean?" Reino asked.

"Went down," I said, and then quoted the research results. "Tons of it disappeared from the ocean in a couple of years."

"Where'd it go?" Reino said.

"Away," I said, and immediately heard the echo of Reino years ago saying that the eagles went away, and Leuty saying the orcas went away.

"Away where?" Reino asked.

I was stumped. The alpha-HCH had raced to the Arctic Ocean. Now that it was not being made, alpha-HCH escaped from the Arctic Ocean. It could not go south when nature was driving it north. Where did it go? My mind raced to gather relevant facts and tidbits. This eighth-grade-educated fisherman was asking penetrating questions—questions Ph.D.'s had not even considered.

"My Inuit friends would probably say that the northern lights ate the alpha-HCH," I finally said, "but I'm guessing that atmospheric chemistry annihilated the alpha-HCH, or it was metabolized in the ocean."

"That atmospheric chemistry and metabolism was always there, wasn't it?" Reino asked.

"What do you mean?" I asked.

"While alpha-HCH was being used, it was also being degraded," Reino said. "It didn't suddenly start degrading when the use stopped."

What insight, I thought. During the period of alpha-HCH use, Arctic atmospheric chemistry and ocean metabolism were present, but the rate of alpha-HCH transfer to the Arctic exceeded the ability of nature to degrade it. The result was an increase of alpha-HCH concentration in the Arctic Ocean. Now, without a continuing source, the degradation processes in the atmosphere and the ocean were greater than the supply, and the ocean was being depleted of alpha-HCH.

The degradation rate of POPs is significant. They are not eternally persistent like mercury or lead. They have environmental fates other than entering the food chain. POPs can be taken out of the active environment by falling into sediments, being metabolized by biota at any level from microorganism to polar bear, captured in ice or tundra, or degraded in the atmosphere. For alpha-HCH, the degradation rate was significant.

Expanding on Uncle Reino's insight, I thought about toxaphene. It is considered to be resistant to atmospheric chemistry, but sensitive to aquatic biota. Remember, when the fish in pristine mountain lakes were purposefully eradicated with toxaphene, the water remained toxic for a longer period of time than it did in warmer, more fertile lakes. Toxaphene was being degraded or being made unavailable in fertile lakes, but in clear, cold waters it remained deadly. The fertile lower Great Lakes are an effective disposal machine for toxaphene.

This was great news. POPs, though persistent, were not 100 percent persistent. They would degrade in the environment, and if their sources were eliminated, they would disappear from the environment and not stagnate like the PCBs and toxaphene in Lake Superior. If POPs were no longer used, why were they not disappearing from the Arctic Ocean and Lake Superior?

Given the capability of the environment to degrade alpha-HCH and toxaphene, it is comfortable to assume that there are large quantities of POPs entering the Northern Hemisphere's airshed. Without a tremendous loading to the environment, the concentration of PCBs over Bermuda could not remain at 76,000 molecules per cubic centimeter after their banning, Lake Superior would not have near constant concentrations of PCBs for decades, and the levels of chlordane, toxaphene, and PCBs in the Arctic Ocean would trend down like those of alpha-HCH if their supply were cut off. Unfortunately, alpha-HCH was the only POP eliminated. All of the others would need to be banned—an unlikely event in countries without regulations.

The POPs model of environmental activists, the USEPA, and the North American scientists is that of indestructible POPs circulating in the environment. The small amount of them entering sediments, being metabolized, or meeting another fate are being replaced by leakage from dump sites or chlorine chemistry gone awry. This model fits the needs of the U.S. regulatory, science, and activist community to have all emissions coming from sources under the EPA's control, but it is far removed from reality.

Unfortunately, the eternally persistent POPs model is also embraced by the United Nations Environmental Programme's (UNEP) effort in global POPs banning. A UNEP report from 2000 still refers to a 1996 UNEP survey indicating no global production of PCBs, 2,070 metric tons (MT=2,200 U.S.

pounds) of DDT, 241.4 MT of toxaphene, and 5.2 MT of Aldrin/Dieldrin. That's all—no chlordane, heptachlor, hexachlorobenzene, or HCH! This survey was based on "responses from sixty governments representing 75% of the worldwide chemical trade." Unfortunately, the countries supplying data are countries that have banned or restricted POPs. The rapidly developing countries making and using POPs are countries that do not share data on chemicals manufactured or used within their borders. Somehow, even Russia's earlier admission of PCB use was not acknowledged in the 2000 UNEP report.

Politically, neither the EPA nor the UNEP wish to identify sources outside of the developed countries, and the developed countries are the only political entities that will respond to environmental concerns. That may be politically correct, but it's scientifically short-sighted. Waste leakage and errant chemistry from developed countries cannot sustain the deadly POPs levels in our cold, clear northern waters.

A careful look at the fate of POPs, with help from Uncle Reino, pointed to the necessary existence of a large source of POPs. This source would have to be near the magnitude of their pre-banning use. What could possibly be so large?

GLOBAL USE

Fortunately, some scientists from Environment Canada were skeptical of the highly persistent POPs model and sought significant continuing sources.[1] They calculated pesticide use rates from the acreage of crops under tillage in countries known to be using POPs, and estimated global use of 1.3 million metric tons of toxaphene prior to 1993. From 1964 until it was totally banned in 1985, the United States used 321,000 metric tons of toxaphene. From research estimates, the developing world's use of toxaphene had far eclipsed U.S. historical uses. Developing countries' use of lindane, chlordane, and DDT was also estimated in the range of hundreds of thousands of metric tons per year. This was significant! Was global agriculture continuing to supply the amount of POPs initially supplied by North America and Europe?

I grew up with the notion that the U.S. and Canadian prairies were the "breadbasket to the world." I'd seen the gigantic grain elevators of Thunder Bay,

---

1. Li Y. F. Global gridded technical HCH-usage inventories using global cropland as a surrogate. See *Journal of Geophysical Research D: Atmospheres* 104, no. 19 (20 October 1999), and earlier papers by this author.

Ontario, loading freighters to transport grain from the Canadian prairies across Lake Superior and down the lakes. North America exported food to nations rich in population and poor in agricultural productivity. If the United States and Canada were the major farming countries and we banned POPs, would uses in the rest of the world be of any consequence? Yet in recent years, farmers couldn't sell what they could produce and were paid to not farm. What in the world was happening?

North American farming technology had revolutionized the developing world's agricultural productivity. Norman Borlaug, the acknowledged creator of this Green Revolution, was born on an Iowa farm in 1914 and joined a Rockefeller Foundation program to research Mexican wheat production in 1944. By 1960, he had developed high-yield disease-resistant dwarf wheat varieties that adapted to a variety of growing conditions. Wheat production in Mexico and Latin America experienced a spectacular increase.

In the 1960s, he brought his technology to India and Pakistan, and in 1970 Norman Borlaug was awarded the Nobel Peace Prize for his humanitarian efforts in averting India and Pakistan's hunger crisis. He continued to work in the Middle East, Asia, and Africa, with spectacular results wherever the technology was introduced. In the last forty years of the twentieth century, worldwide wheat production went from 300 to 600 million metric tons, and the developing world began feeding itself. During that time, India increased wheat production from 12 to 76 million metric tons, and Pakistan went from 4.5 to 21 million metric tons. The revolution spread to other countries and other grains to create breadbaskets of production in Asia and the Middle East, allowing once starving nations to become agricultural exporters.

The high-yield agriculture of the Green Revolution requires genetically superior seeds, fertilizer, water, and pesticides. As the production of wheat and other grains moved into developing countries, the pesticides of the time, POPs, went along as part of the package. In the midst of preventing human starvation, the potential wildlife and human health problems from North American POPs experience were not a priority.

POPs use flourished in countries participating in this growing global agricultural revolution. No wonder my industrial friend was excited about the business opportunity to make toxaphene in China, and an agricultural researcher friend described toxaphene as "the most widely used pesticide on the planet." U.S. farmers did not give up toxaphene without a fight, and a fight to ban a cheap and effective pesticide would not even get started in a developing country.

No wonder the concentrations of POPs pesticides in the Arctic were static. While they were being banned in North America and Europe, their use rate was increasing in developing countries. The global transport of POPs pesticides to the Arctic and their refusal to disappear was finally making sense, but how did this relate to PCBs and Lake Superior?

My major concern, and the reason I started this search, was that following North America's ban of PCBs, their concentration in Lake Superior decreased to 50 percent of peak levels and then stagnated. I found that PCB levels in the air above Bermuda stayed constant at 76,000 molecules per cubic centimeter for decades.[2] According to the AMAP study, PCBs in Lake Superior were at expected levels when compared to levels in large freshwater lakes in northern Canada. In the Lake Michigan Mass Balance study, PCBs were venting from the lake faster than they were depositing from the air. Now, PCBs were found in the mid-Pacific—and, it seemed, everywhere they were sought.

From Soren Jensen's 1960s studies on pike in lakes of northern Sweden, to the finding of PCBs in a remote lake on Lake Superior's Isle Royale in the 1970s, to their discovery on an ice island in the 1980s, it was apparent that PCBs traveled through the air to all parts of the world. The previously referenced paper on global distillation provided convincing evidence that PCBs and other POPs moved through the atmosphere from the equator toward the poles. It was clear that PCBs were present in the environment and moving through the air, but what was sustaining their presence? Logically, PCBs like alpha-HCH would be subjected to atmospheric degradation and other environmental fates. If there was no PCB addition to the global environment, one would assume that the contamination levels would decrease. A major source of global PCB emissions is needed to sustain its presence in the Northern Hemisphere.

Russian negotiators to the UNEP POPs-banning sessions admitted historical and continuing PCB use. We found this surprising, but in thinking about the fight to ban PCBs in the United States, it should not be surprising that developing nations did not ban PCBs. Why would Russia, China,

---

2. Ronald A. Hites, "Global Atmospheric Behavior of Polychlorinated Biphenyls," 6 October 1999, http://nigec.ucdavis.edu/publications/annual95/midwestern/project04.html.

India, and other nations currently on a pollution growth curve matching that of North America in the 1960s ban PCBs? It is more reasonable to assume that PCBs are still used and abused in the developing economies. When that assumption is accepted, all other behaviors of PCBs on the planet make sense. If PCBs had been globally banned in the 1980s, global concentrations would be rapidly decreasing, not stagnant.

Alpha-HCH entered the Arctic Ocean when its global use rate over-whelmed its natural destruction rate, and then vented from the Arctic Ocean when global use ceased. What is this natural destruction? Will it destroy all POPs? Let's take a closer look at the destruction of POPs in the environment.

NATURAL DESTRUCTION

Earth's troposphere, the seven-mile-thick blanket of air surrounding us, is a powerful chemical reactor. Radiation from the sun attacks oxygen and oxides of nitrogen to create ozone and highly reactive oxygen, hydroxyl, and chlorine radicals to reduce compounds of carbon, hydrogen, and chlorine to carbon dioxide, water, and hydrochloric acid. To better understand this chemical reactor and its affect on POPs, let's take a look at a group of chemicals that escaped destruction in the troposphere.

In 1968 the use of chlorofluorocarbons (CFCs) reached a peak of 2.5 billion pounds per year, a much greater amount than all of the global POPs combined. CFCs were used for solvents, refrigerants, and pressure-can propellants for everything from paint to perfume. CFCs are compounds of carbon, chlorine, and fluorine. The carbon-to-chorine or fluorine bond is very stable, so CFCs are not attacked by the tropospheric chemical reactor. CFCs are very volatile, not water-soluble, and disperse throughout the global atmosphere like oxygen and nitrogen.

Scientists wondered what the environmental fate of CFCs would be, and were surprised to find that they remained in the atmosphere. Increased production and use continued to increase their atmospheric concentration. The stable CFCs diffused into the stratosphere, the atmospheric layer above the troposphere. Ozone in the stratosphere adsorbs high-energy emissions from the sun to protect life, as we know it, on earth.

The high-energy radiation in the stratosphere is strong enough to rupture a carbon-to-chlorine bond. When CFCs in the stratosphere are attacked, the resulting chlorine radicals each initiate chain reactions to destroy thousands of ozone molecules. Depletion of stratospheric ozone led to the phasing-out of CFC production and use according to the Montreal Protocol of 1989. CFCs are being replaced by HCFCs, compounds containing at least one atom of hydrogen. This carbon-to-hydrogen bond will be broken in the troposphere, allowing removal of the HCFCs and protection of stratospheric ozone.

The troposphere abhors a carbon-to-hydrogen bond, a feature of all POPs except hexachlorobenzene. The same chemistry that keeps HCFCs out of the atmosphere should remove POPs. How fast?

The U.S. Department of Health and Human Services' Agency for Toxic Substance and Disease Registry (ATSDR) has produced extensive peer-reviewed profiles of the POPs and other chemicals.[3] These profiles provide scientific data on POPs, including environmental concentrations and fate. In ATSDR's profile, toxaphene was found to be rather resistant to atmospheric degradation, but more susceptible to metabolism in the food chain than other POPs.

Other major POPs have surprisingly short half-lives in the troposphere. Using a method of calculating the half-life of chemicals from structure, chlordane vapor in the troposphere would have an expected half-life of 1.3 days. The half-life of PCBs is dependent upon their degree of chlorination, with the tetra- and penta-chloro congeners having a half-life of weeks and the less chlorinated isomers measured in days. DDT's atmospheric half-life is estimated at two days and Dieldrin's at one day. These values are theoretical; they are "calculated" from laboratory observations on model systems. The profiles explained that real-life degradation rates could be slower than calculated, and POPs adsorbed to particles would be protected from atmospheric chemistry. If the rates were dozens of times slower, it would still take a major input of POPs to maintain the static POPs levels in the environment.

Lindane, gamma-HCH, was found to have limited response to atmospheric chemistry, but was degraded by algae and in natural lake water, where its half-life was only a few days. Alpha-HCH probably suffered an aquatic fate in the Arctic Ocean. Somehow, the processes of nature give Earth a "carrying capacity" for almost anything, even chemicals with the persistency of POPs.

The puzzle of source, transport, and fate of POPs is finally fitting together. The growing economies of the world are the continuing source;

---

3. For example, "Toxicological Profile for Chlordane (Update)," USDH&HS, Public Health Service, Agency for Toxic Substances and Disease Registry, TP-93/03, is a 234-page, 1994-issued update of a 1989 chlordane profile.

POPs are transported by air; and they succumb to chemical degradation in their transporting air, and biotic degradation in the waters they enter. The whole picture would seem like a beautiful symphony of natural interactions if the effect of the surviving POPs on wildlife and humans were not so deadly. Let's join a POP for a global journey.

GLOBAL TRANSPORT

Every year, when the sun returns to Antarctica, the "ozone hole" is re-created. When I see the latest version on national news, I think how wonderful it would be to visualize the seasonal dumping of pesticides onto fields on one side of the globe and their dispersal around the world.

Lacking the millions of dollars worth of satellite data-gathering technology and graphics programs, I imagine myself as a toxaphene molecule sprayed onto some cropland in southern India. I land on an advantageous perch, the underside of a leaf, and view the fate of my fellow molecules while wondering what will happen to me.

A small percentage of my brothers enter pests, joining the food chain when a bird eats their dead pest. A rain washes other brothers away, but I manage to cling to my perch.

On an especially hot day, I evaporate from my tightly packed matrix of toxaphene brothers and enter the air. I'm much heavier than an oxygen or nitrogen molecule, but once evaporated, I have no tendency to fall to the ground. My driving force is to diffuse away from the high concentration of toxaphene molecules in this farmland area. The air is crowded with a mixture of hundreds of thousands of POPs per cubic centimeter, bumping into each other and attempting to diffuse away from their brothers. Every known POP and their families of isomers, congeners, and impurities are present. What a great place to "POPs watch"!

Diffusion and air currents push me higher and higher. Particles of smoke, soil, sea salt, desert sand, pollen, smelter ash, and all manner of unidentified dusts float along with the rising air. I join brothers adsorbed to particles, spending about 20 percent of my time on a particle and 80 percent in the air. I visit PCBs and other pesticides in the air and on particles. Dioxin molecules, the least volatile of the POPs, are rarely seen, and almost always on a particle. The lighter and faster HCH molecules avoid particles.

Over a large industrial city, the sunlight-induced atmospheric chemistry is enhanced by a yellowish cloud of nitrogen oxide and hydrocarbon emissions. An army of hydroxyl radicals, oxygen radicals, chlorine radicals, and ozone molecules takes a toll on all POPs. My toxaphene family, the HCH isomers, and the hexachlorobenzenes (HCBs) are rather immune to atmospheric chemistry, but we all lose a few brothers in the dense smog of polluted air.

As the air mass rises, I get cold. At the colder temperature, I spend 50 percent of my time adsorbed to one particle or another. I spend longer times on particles that like me and hold me close. I look down and realize that when we spend more time on particles, we are decreasing our air concentration and urging more brothers to come up. All of the POPs and their impurities are concentrating on particles, jumping off now and then, moving higher and getting cooler. Cold does not bother us, so moving along in the mass of air, watching the scenery below, is a real party.

The water vapor rising from the sun-baked land begins to condense into clouds. The current I am riding is lifted by the warm humid air. I ride a particle up between groups of cumulus clouds composed of tiny particles surrounded by condensed water. I am just reaching the top of the cloud layer when, zap!—it suddenly gets wet and warmed a bit as water vapor condenses around my particle. I am stuck in a cloud droplet along with a group of brothers and POPs friends. The droplet cools, and after quite some time, I diffuse to its surface and trade places with a brother coming in from the air. I am above the clouds enjoying the new scenery when I get caught in the violent updraft of an approaching weather front and am swept higher and higher. It also gets colder and colder, so I latch onto a crowded particle, finding myself spending 80 percent of my time on particles at the colder temperatures. I continue up in the massive, growing system until I again feel that momentary warming, wet sensation and am again encased in a droplet. This time it gets really cold as we bolt for the top of the troposphere in the middle of a dark, anvil-shaped cumulonimbus storm cloud. With the sudden creation of billions of water droplets, I find more room in mine, and more brothers come in from the air. My droplet bumps into another droplet, and we join together. After a few more collisions, my drop with its bundle of particles is growing, getting heavier, and beginning to fall. All around me, large drops of rain are falling. We are hit by one from above and grow even bigger, falling faster. My drop hits the ground with a splat.

We fall into a field near the ocean and I stay with my particle. I am swept into a river where I am pushed off by a stranger, an organic contaminant that sticks tightly to my particle. A few of my brothers are on particles that hold them so tight that they go out to sea, settle into sediments, and are buried. Their journey is delayed. Others are ingested by microscopic organisms or bottom-feeding fish and mollusks, getting metabolized or having their journey delayed. I stay in the water most of the time, visiting a particle once in a while, as I ride an ocean current for two days. I finally reach the surface and evaporate into the air.

A tropical easterly carries me across Africa. It is a dry flight, and the scenery is fantastic. I spend most of my time in the air, but enjoy visiting particles, talking with many brothers, and sharing experiences. Some have traveled for months, moving generally north and then getting sent back in an unusual weather event, giving them several trips around the world. They talk about thousands of brothers that have moved on. I ask if "moving on" means termination. They assure me that most of us toxaphene molecules avoid termination and move north. One old timer, who has been traveling a long time, says he'd been in the food chain. He was in the dark for years, moving from a crowded environment to a more crowded one until he finally escaped from a dead whale.

One PCB molecule made it to the Arctic, was taken up by a bird feeding on the minnow he was in, and returned south in the migrating bird. Another rode a bird north and escaped when its thin-shelled egg cracked on laying.

I enjoy the dry trip, and hope I can avoid the food chain on this venture to wherever north is. West of Africa, I get caught up in a weather system transporting energy north. After a few dunks in the ocean, I join a tropical depression for a long, wet, and stormy trip across the Atlantic. I end up being deposited in Belize. On the next leg, I join an easterly air mass that moves over the Gulf of Mexico and up into the United States, where I am dumped into Lake Superior for a short stop. According to the seasoned toxaphene travelers, we are lucky to land in the clear northern lakes, because the chance of getting into the food chain or tied up in organic sediments is much higher in the southern Great Lakes or warmer inland lakes that are full of hungry living things.

The next time I reach higher altitudes it is really cold, and when I suddenly feel a warming, I am surrounded but I'm not wet. I am trapped in an ice crystal that has been rapidly building into a snowflake that eventually falls onto the tundra of northern Quebec. Veteran brothers comfort me, telling me that with winter setting in, it might be a while, but I'll be released. They encourage me to avoid getting trapped on the tundra, because it could grow over us and bury us for good. They have visited Greenland, where brothers have gotten buried under snow and eventually trapped in glaciers.

I am fortunate to be swept into Hudson Strait in a spring rain. I have been riding a friendly but not tightly gripping particle near the surface, eager to jump off into the air, when suddenly we are surrounded by a cloud of plankton. My particle is ingested and the world goes black; toxaphene brothers and POPs friends surround me in a dense fluid. "Welcome to the food chain," a brother says. "Been here before?" "No," I say. "Will I get out?" "I've been here several times," he says. "Most of us will get out, but it'll be a while—a long while."

Conditions keep getting worse as the plankton ingest more particles and POPs. I ask the experienced brother why we can't diffuse out of this crowded place. "We're trapped," he says. "We're stuck in the fat." There is a deafening crunch and the fat globule is released, rolling around in a dark cavern. "Are we out?" I ask. "No, just another step up the chain," he says. "Probably a shrimp." The shrimp gorges himself on plankton for a day, growing and packing the POPs tighter and tighter together. There is another loud crunch. "The end of the shrimp?" I ask. "We're part of a small fish now,' the veteran says. "We'll be here a little longer."

The minnow eats shrimp for days. It is good to be in one place for a while, but it keeps getting more crowded. A hungry cod traveling up Baffin Island's east coast eats the minnow, and a pregnant ringed seal eats the cod. I am transferred to her fat-rich milk and into the pup. The brothers and POPs are oppressively close in the hungry pup's fat. Most of us who had gotten into plankton are still surviving, and I am beginning to think the few who have been metabolized are lucky.

My seal pup is eaten by a young male walrus, who then wanders the north for two years, living on mollusks and feasting on seal and narwhal pups along the edge of the ice. He is a large and beautiful specimen, but an unsuccessful breeder. He is driven away by females and forced to live at the edge of the walrus colony, or alone. I spend a long time in his POPs-crowded fat and am glad to hear him go dormant after a long fight with a polar bear.

My thoughts of escape are shattered when my fat globule is eaten by a female polar bear that has pushed a gorging male aside.

The polar bears mate, and I am in the female's fat during hibernation. The living conditions are harsh. I am being squashed by the increasing concentration of my brothers and the billions of toxaphene impurities around me, pounded by the rapidly moving HCH molecules fighting for their space, and I count 118 of the 209 congeners of PCBs while pinned between a DDT molecule and six chlordane impurities. I find myself squeezed into the bear's bloodstream, where I watch PCB congeners, my toxaphene brothers, and chlordane isomers wrestle with her endocrines and other chemical messengers. A single cub is born, and its nursing removes much of its mother's fat, bringing us POPs oppressively close as the winter progresses.

While back in her fat, I wait to transfer to her milk, but the nursing stops. The cub has died. The dejected female wanders the ice floes, wondering what was wrong. She doesn't eat and loses fat. I am ready to metabolize to escape the brutal conditions.

The male finds my host without cubs and fights with her. She drives him off and continues her wandering, stumbling into an Inuit hunting encampment. She has lived in the far north and has never encountered humans. She has no fear. The leaping camp dog is disemboweled with one swat of her powerful forepaw, but a rifle bullet destroys her heart.

I am hoping for escape as the Inuk hunter skins my host. My hopes are dashed when he looks longingly at my fat globule and I slide down his throat.

There is no need for extensive models and graphics of the flow of POPs into our waters to understand POPs flow. The problem is very simple: POPs used in the Northern Hemisphere end up in cold, clear northern waters. To remove the toxicity, POPs uses in all countries must be banned. I'm confident of this, but I've had simple ideas before that had big holes in them. I needed to confirm my findings with a spectrum of people.

CONFIRMATION

Personal experiences, extensive travel, meetings, and sorting through decades of research brought me to the startling conclusion that developing countries were polluting all cold, clear northern waters. Local banning of POPs resulted in diminished local and regional concentrations, but a background global contamination remains. As long as global uses of hundreds of thousands of tons per year flood the Northern Hemisphere's atmosphere, our cold and clear waters will remain deadly. I saw no flaws in the logic bringing me to this conclusion and sought the verification of independent experts.

Many of the chemists and engineers I had worked with during the 1960s were retired, and now active in environmental organizations and causes. I presented them the case for nonpolar, semivolatile compounds of limited water solubility traveling to the Arctic and depositing in the Great Lakes along the way in a "Could this be possible?" manner. To a person, they looked at me as though I'd lost my mind. Then they thought. Within minutes, they would slap their foreheads and say, "Why didn't I think of that?"

An agricultural-marketing friend confirmed that agriculture in developing countries had no reason to abandon POPs pesticides. He was an environmentally sensitive person who had lived through the developed countries' transition away from POPs pesticides, but would not have thought of their continuing use in developing countries without being prompted. For some reason, the idea that foreign countries pollute our air and water is . . . well . . . foreign.

During my Arctic travels, I'd maintained contact with the Michigan Audubon Society and shared my experiences in their newsletter. I sent an early draft of my global-transport thoughts to Audubon's Michael Boyce, an old friend who had been the Great Lakes Regional Corporate Environmental Counsel's (GLRCEC) staff person in its waning years. Mike called back to congratulate me on the effort and asked if he could send it to Jim Ludwig.

Dr. Ludwig was the ecotoxicologist who had taught me about POPs in the environment, but we had parted company during the chlorine war. He supported the banning of chlorine in an impassioned paper, stating it was necessary to "protect the children." I wondered how children could be protected without chlorinated drinking water. I'd last seen him at the final GLRCEC meeting and heard of his findings of PCB-compromised albatrosses near abandoned military sites in the far Pacific. Now I was advocating global banning of POPs to "protect the children" of the Inuit.

I knew that Jim went to the Pacific to implicate the military bases and force their cleanup, and thought back to the people still believing that old DEW Line and weather-station installations were responsible for Broughton Island's contaminated marine food chain. Getting Jim to believe that foreign chemicals were polluting North American waters was as likely as getting the USEPA to believe that POPs flowed into the United States from across oceans and borders. I remembered Jim's excellent help in finding POPs in our pond, and other positive interactions. I desired his honest assessment and told Mike to send him my draft.

Jim responded with a hearty and astonishing "Good work, old friend. We have been traveling separate paths and came to the same conclusion. Let's get together and make sure this truth gets spread."

When Jim and his cohorts studied the far Pacific, they found contamination to be general to the ocean and not emanating from the military installations. Further research was implicating high concentrations of POPs in the air over eastern Asia.

The POPs pendulum definitely made wide swings between Jim and me. We started on opposite poles, came together with GLRCEC, swung away again in the chlorine war, and now after years of independent POPs study were back together.

Jim was concerned about another swinging pendulum.

After the International Joint Commission's chlorine-ban debacle, the Great Lakes protection agenda and research-support dollars moved toward the ecosystem agenda championed by SOLEC, the organization described on page 63. In the early 1990s, the fact that POPs were affecting wildlife at fractions of the levels then present in the lakes was unfolding to IJC scientists. This finding encouraged them to support a chlorine ban that backfired; its researchers were left with toxic lakes and no funding.

Jim Ludwig flooded me with research papers and advice. It was good to have a "friend in the business" to navigate through the complexity of a field I do not understand. The bottom line I received is that in just a brief look at PCBs, toxicologists have found an amazing and scary number of ways that specific congeners and their metabolites can cause harm to life. In looking at only PCBs, there are more unknowns than knowns, and to totally understand their effect in the environment would take decades, and billions of dollars.

That's just PCBs, the industrial-chemical POP. Now, think about the pesticide POPs. They were made to kill, and when their targeted victims adapted to their poisoning, another generation of POPs was introduced. Sorting out the effects of only toxaphene and its 670 impurities would be impossible.

Life in Earth's clear, cold waters is on the edge. The chance of it getting worse with the introduction of a new POP, or increased use of an existing POP, is more likely than the chance of POPs use reduction.

Obtaining the opinions of trusted old friends with a spectrum of chemical and environmental convictions taught me that POPs are doing more damage than I thought. I'm convinced of the need to globally ban POPs, but where do we go for help? None of the current efforts are going to solve the POPs dilemma.

POPS DILEMMA

In the 1960s, Rachel Carson's *Silent Spring* taught us that killing our air, lakes, and wildlife was not a necessary price of progress. Shortly thereafter, we began the banning of POPs, and their environmental concentrations declined rapidly . . . for a short period of time.

In 1989, environmental activists and the International Joint Commission expressed their outrage over the continuing presence of POPs by recommending Zero Discharge. By 1991, they were willing to ban chlorine to keep POPs from the Great Lakes Basin. In spite of significant North American efforts, dangerous POPs levels still linger in air and cold, clear waters from the United States to the Arctic Ocean.

Environmental activism, regulation, and dollars did a good job of eliminating regional POPs use. Additional activism such as the Zero Discharge and chlorine-ban attempts, regulation such as Pollution Prevention efforts, and billions of dollars to remove sediments from lakes and rivers did not and will not result in significant future gains.

For the first time in the development and imposition of environmental solutions, our governmental agencies are of no help. The combined might of the USEPA and Environment Canada is incapable of making a dent in the current dangerous POPs levels. Unfortunately, that does not stop them from trying. They will continue to pin their hopes on taking POPs out of our waters by removing POPs-contaminated sediments, an approach that serves only to deflect attention from the real cause: foreign uses that they cannot control and will not recognize.

Environmental activists are also frustrated by the contamination of our air and waters by foreign sources. It is counterintuitive to their assumption that we arrogant North Americans are always taking advantage of the undeveloped world. It also flies in the face of their mantras—"Think Globally and Act Locally," or the old Pogo comic strip's "We have met the Enemy and He is Us." It will be difficult for most environmental activists to raise money to rally against pesticide-using peasants in the developing world.

The United Nations Environmental Programme has made a valiant attempt to obtain an international POPs ban. So far, actions under this initiative have been limited to the expensive cleanup of an oversupply of POPs to undeveloped countries, and educational programs to reduce the formation of dioxin. True POPs elimination is voluntary and gives targets of around 2025. Our planet has had a voluntary nuclear-disarmament agreement for about twenty-five years, but there has been no progress. There is no reason to expect progress in POPs reduction from the UNEP agreement.

No current effort addresses the real problem: the use of hundreds of thousands of tons of persistent pesticides and PCBs by developing countries. Is there any hope?

There'd better be hope. I'm tired of breathing toxic air, and hope that you are too. I want my grandchildren and the Inuit to be able to freely consume the delicacies from our cold, clear northern waters. It's time to wake up the troops and get into action.

ACTION

AWARENESS

Unfortunately, waking up the troops to rally against POPs use is not the first step. There are no troops. We need to recruit them, and that task has been made difficult by our governments' desire to keep the lid on POPs as a problem. Inuit are told there is no significant harm from POPs, and our state and provincial governments reduce the toxicity of fish in our lakes by not measuring the most toxic component. We are expected to believe that if industry stops emitting those unrelated "air toxics," POPs will disappear, and if we dredge our lakes and rivers free of toxic sediments, the water will be POPs-free . . . have patience. My patience is gone, and I hope yours is too.

If we in the developed world are unaware of the source of POPs poisoning of our air and water, think of the level of awareness of the users in developing nations. I was a chemical manufacturer in a developing nation forty years ago, and I had no awareness of the pollution caused by my chemicals. I cannot imagine that any level of awareness of POPs pollution exists in more than a handful of people in the current developing countries.

If you went to see your congressperson or senator to ask their help in getting immediate POPs-banning action by the developing countries, they would probably wish you would go away and not bring more complexities to the international agenda of human rights, terrorist activities, global trade, global warming, and a host of other priorities. If interested, or faking it to please you, they'd ask how large your constituency was. How many votes do you represent? Is your topic reflected in my polls?

Creating an awareness of the source, transport, fate, and effect of POPs use is critical to obtaining action through any channel. In North America or developing countries, without awareness nothing will happen.

In order to recruit and wake up troops, clear and understandable marching orders are needed as a message. What message should we send?

THE MESSAGE

Whenever POPs elimination is discussed, a variety of confounding issues arise. How can we ban DDT? Malaria will return. What about dioxin, the most toxic of all POPs—shouldn't it be addressed first? How will we dispose of existing stocks without contaminating the environment? The emerging brominated and fluorinated POPs need to be assessed and addressed. Shouldn't all pesticides be eliminated?

All of the above issues are worthy of concern, but their current effect on the deadliness of our cold and clear waters is not comparable to that of PCBs and POPs pesticides. These POPs are the major problem, and there are substitutes for them. The developed world has been free of these POPs for decades.

In the United States and Canada, POPs were quickly eliminated. POPs elimination is not technologically complex or economically infeasible. Effective replacement technology exists. There is no reason for continued PCB use in industry or POPs pesticides in agriculture. None!

The message is simple. POPs used anywhere in the Northern Hemisphere travel through the air; contaminate our cold, clear waters; bioaccumulate up the food chain; and wreak havoc with wildlife and humans. Most of the toxicity comes from the agricultural use of chlordane and toxaphene. Manufacture and import of these chemicals should cease immediately. Use of existing stocks for two years would be acceptable.

Following the ban of chlordane and toxaphene, all other POPs pesticide use in agriculture, and all uses of PCBs, should be banned.

The message is straightforward and simple. Is the timing right?

TIME FOR CHANGE

London burned soft coal until people died in the streets. North America killed its lakes and birds until Rachel Carson eloquently questioned pollution as a necessary price of progress. Now, the developing nations are polluting at will and sending chemicals we banned back to us. Is it time for the developing countries to change? From our perspective it is, but can we dictate change to others?

Current leadership of the developed world is not likely to champion a global POPs ban. POPs banning will not make the agenda of the Group of Eight when it meets to discuss the problems and opportunities of global business. It is more likely that the current POPs users will decide for themselves to ban POPs.

As the year 2005 came to a close, the environmental attitude in China showed evidence of change. Two chemicals spills were reported on international TV, and we saw people being supplied with bottled water, and technicians sampling the receiving river. Russia was notified of the plume's progress toward them. These were not the first spills, but certainly the first evidence of concern. How many Asians know that their agricultural practices are polluting waters around the world? The people of all developing countries might just be as ready for change as we were in the 1960s if they knew that for very little personal advantage, they are causing the deterioration of their health and Arctic wildlife. How can they be informed, convinced, and persuaded to act? Is there a budding Rachel Carson in their midst?

How can we recruit and wake up troops in developing countries?

ACTION

Unfortunately, we do not have a global leader who will say the POPs equivalent of President Reagan's "Mr. Gorbachev, tear down that wall." And there are none on the horizon as they all fight for their own survival in the "post-cold-war era" global economy.

The POPs-using developing countries are strong participants in this global economy, supplying us technical expertise through optical fiber phone lines, and ships and planes full of a spectrum of goods that fill our store shelves. Their belching smokestacks are reminiscent of North America in the 1950s as they produce a three-kilometer-thick "Asian Brown Cloud" that blocks the sun and cools the ground it shades. As we did in the 1950s, they perceive pollution as the price of progress and resist outside suggestions to sacrifice progress for our cleaner air and water. We lack global leadership that is capable of solving the POPs problem, but we may have an alarm clock that can wake up the troops.

That marvelous communication tool called the Internet has made global business flourish. Money, information, and technology now flow around the world to allow anyone in a stable country to become a global supplier of goods and services. That same tool can be used to inform our suppliers in developing countries that we appreciate their low-cost and high-quality goods and services, but we do not want to breathe any more of their persistent and toxic chemicals or have our waters polluted.

I wish that I could give you a magical e-mail address to send a note demanding the cessation of POPs-pesticide and PCB use, but I do not know one. Lacking that capability, I suggest mass action by passing the POPs story on to everyone you know, with the objective of getting the truth to millions of people in North America, Europe, and Asia who are sick of breathing toxics and not being able to eat food from our cold, clear waters. In time, with the citizenry of developed and developing countries expressing a desire for POPs elimination, our leadership will follow. Their polls will tell them to. With your help, it might happen in time to bring back Gloria's eagle.

GLORIA'S EAGLE

In the mid-1990s, I launched my kayak from our condo on Portage Lake in Hancock, Michigan, and asked Gloria to pick me up at McLain's Park, the spot where I had spent my first night in the Copper Country. Late in the ten-mile paddle, nearing Lake Superior, I heard screeching and stopped to listen. The sound came from an eagle's nest in a white pine sticking out above the forest canopy. It was the first nest I had seen near the Lake Superior shores.

Eagles were making their way back into Michigan and successfully breeding inland on a diet of terrestrial animals. Nests near Great Lakes shores produced either no young, or chicks with crossed beaks or clubbed feet. In the interior of Michigan's Upper Peninsula, eagles were frequently seen with ravens on road kill. It was heartening to hear the young screeching for food in a nest near the lake. I hoped they were healthy.

Gloria and I frequented this spot in our runabout. We would kill the engine and rest for a while, watching the nest. On one trip with my daughter and granddaughters, we were treated to a doe and two fawns cavorting along the shoreline. Sometimes I did not see the eagle parents, but whenever Gloria was along, a majestic adult awaited us from the top of a dead cedar. I called it "Gloria's eagle."

We watched the young leave the nest and soar above the trees. The nest was successful for several years. In 2003, we began to see the eagles closer to town and watched them eating scraps and trimmings from the Indian fish-processing plant.

In 2005, I did not see any eagles on an early trip, and when passing the area in late July on a sailing trip to Isle Royale, they were not there. On the return from Isle Royale, the nest was empty. I asked around and found there were no eagles on the nest at any time. They might have been hit by a car while on road kill, a common death in upper Michigan, but I know that regular feeding at the processing plant would bring a sufficient increase in dietary POPs to cause breeding failure and nest abandonment. I feared that as their fate . . . all for a free lunch.

The greatest of lakes is the cleanest of the Great Lakes, but its life-supporting ability rests on a ragged edge. Start the ball rolling to clear our air and give all waters of the Northern Hemisphere a chance. Make a difference by spreading the POPs story as fast and as far as you can. Please visit the weblog www.coldclearandeadly.com for the latest or to express your opinion.

SUGGESTED READING

BOOKS

Ashworth, William. *The Late Great Lakes: An Environmental History.* Detroit: Wayne State University Press, 1987.

Colburn, Theo. *Our Stolen Future: Are We Threatening Our Fertility, Intelligence, and Survival?: A Scientific Detective Story.* New York: Dutton, 1996.

Cone, Marla. *Silent Snow: The Slow Poisoning of the Arctic.* New York: Grove Press, 2004.

Dempsey, Dave. *On the Brink: The Great Lakes in the 21st Century.* East Lansing: Michigan State University Press, 2004.

Dempsey, Dave. *Ruin and Recovery: Michigan's Rise as a Conservation Leader.* Ann Arbor: The University of Michigan Press, 2001.

Freuchen, Peter, and Finn Salomonsen. *The Arctic Year.* New York: Putnam, 1958.

Olsen, Marco A. *Analysis of the Stockholm Convention on Persistent Organic Pollutants.* Dobbs Ferry: Oceana Publications, Inc., 2003.

Ramamoorthy and Ramamoorthy. *Chlorinated Organic Chemicals in the Environment,* Boca Raton: CRC Press, 1997.

Scherman, Katharine. *Spring on an Arctic Island.* Boston: Little, Brown, 1956.

Suzuki, David. *A Lifetime of Ideas from a Leading Activist and Thinker.* Edmond: Greystone Press, 2003.

Whelan, Dr. Elizabeth. *Toxic Terror.* Ottawa: Jameson Books, 1989.

REPORTS

AMAP, 1997. *Arctic Pollution Issues: A State of the Arctic Environment Report.* Arctic Monitoring and Assessment Programme (AMAP), Oslo, Norway. xii+188 pp., http://www.amap.no.

AMAP, 1998. *AMAP Assessment Report: Arctic Pollution Issues.* Arctic Monitoring and Assessment Programme (AMAP), Oslo, Norway. xii+859 pp., http://www.amap.no/.

Center for Indigenous Peoples' Nutrition and Environment (CINE). *Assessment of Dietary Benefit/Risk in Inuit Communities.* McGill University, August 2000. (This is the report of a very extensive study of Inuit uptake of nutrition and toxics from their marine diet.)

Great Waters Program. *Relative Atmospheric Loadings of Toxic contaminants and Nitrogen to the Great Waters.* Office of Air Quality and Standards, USEPA.

Journal of Toxicology and Environmental Health, Special Issue: International Joint Commission Workshop on Cause-Effect Linkages 33, no. 4 (1991).

Michigan Audubon Society, 1991. *Cause-Effect Linkages II Symposium Abstracts,* ed. Steve Schneider and Rick Campbell

U.S. Department of Health and Human Services. *Toxicological Profile for [Any POP]* Agency for Toxic Substances and Disease Registry. The PCB profile, updated November 2001, is available at http://www.atsdr.cdc.gov/toxprofiles/tp17.html; all of the POP pesticides profiles are available from this site.

ARTICLES AND PAPERS

Colborn, Theo et al. "Developmental Effects of Endocrine-Disrupting Chemicals in Wildlife and Humans." *Environmental Perspectives* (1993).

Dewailly, Eric et al. "Inuit Exposure to Organochlorines through the Arctic Food Chain in Arctic Quebec." *Environmental Health Perspectives* (1993).

Fein, C. G., Jacobsen, J. L. et al. "Prenatal Exposure To Polychlorinated Biphenyls: Effects On Birth Size And Gestational Age." *The Journal of Pediatrics* (1984).

Harner, Tom. "Organochlorine Contamination of the Canadian Arctic, and Speculation On Future Trends." *International Journal of Environment and Pollution* 8 (1997).

Hite, R. A. *Global Atmospheric Behavior of Polychlorinated Biphenyls.* Midwest Regional Center Progress Reports, July 1, 1994–June 30, 1995. (Describes a PCB study in Bermuda.)

Jacobsen, J. L. and Jacobsen, S. W. "Evidence for PCBs as neurodevelopmental toxicants in humans." *Neurotoxicology* (1997).

Klasson-Weiler, Eva et al. "Hydroxylated and Methylated Polychlorinated Biphenyl Metabolites in Albatrosses from Midway Atoll." *Environmental Toxicological Chemistry* 17 (1998).

Kuhnline, H. V. et al. "Indigenous Women Consume Greater than Acceptable Levels of Organochlorines." *American Institute of Nutrition* (1995).

Landers, D. H. "Airborne Contaminants in the Arctic: What We Need to Know." *The Science of the Total Environment* 160–61 (1995).

Li, Y. F. "Global Technical Hexachlorocyclohexane Use and Its Contamination Consequences in the Environment: From 1948 to 1997." *The Science of the Total Environment* 232, no. 3 (1999).

Ludwig, James P. et al. *A Comparison of Water Quality Criteria for the Great Lakes Based on Human and Wildlife Health.* International Association for Great Lakes Research, 1993.

Ludwig, James P. et al. *Deformities, PCBs, and TCDD-Equivalents in the Double-Crested Cormorants (Phalacrorax auritus) and Caspian Terns (Hydroprogne caspia) of the Upper Great Lakes 1986–1991: Testing a Cause-Effect Hypothesis.* International Association for Great Lakes Research, 1996.

Oehme, M., et al. "Sources and Pathways of Persistent Organic Pollutants to the Remote Areas of The North Atlantic and Levels in the Marine Food Chain. A Research Update." *The Science of the Total Environment* (1996).

Pierce, Fred. "Why Is the Apparently Pristine Arctic Full of Toxic Chemicals that Started Off Thousands of Miles Away?" *New Scientist* (1997).

Raloff, Janet. "The Pesticide Shuffle." *Science News* 149 (1996).

Shane, Barbra S. "Human Reproductive Hazards." *Environmental Science and Technology* 23, no. 10 (1989).

Voldner, Eva C. and Yi-Fan Li. "Global Usage of Selected Persistent Organochlorines." *The Science of the Total Environment* 160–61 (1995).

Wania, Frank and MacKay. "Tracking the Distribution of Persistent Organic Pollutants." *Environmental Science and Technology* 30, no. 9 (1996).

INDEX

acid rain, 114

"active sediments," 159

activists: against chlorine, 37, 44, 49, 50, 51, 53, 55; Commoner as an, 33; environmental, 22; First Nations, 31, 56; at IJC meetings, 31–32, 49, 50, 51, 53, 55–57, 58–59; locked out of meetings, 64; nuclear, 33; and POPs, 175–76; and Zero Discharge, 31, 33, 49, 51, 57, 175. *See also* chlorine

Africa, 76, 89, 157, 164, 170

Agency for Toxic Substance and Disease Registry (ATSDR), 167

Agent Orange, 56

agriculture: and Canada, 163–64; and developing countries, 89–90, 114–15, 160, 163–65, 166, 172, 173, 176, 177–80; Green Revolution, 164; and POPs, 163, 178

airborne contaminants, 33–34, 56, 61, 66, 169–72; in the Arctic, 135–36; in Canada, 66–67; lake sources for, 78–79; POPs, 70, 73, 85, 168; toxaphene, 89, 92, 168

airshed, 135–36, 168–71; Canada, 70; Great Lakes, 67–70, 83; Lake Michigan, 76–77, 78, 80; Lake Superior, 114; PCBs in the, 95; POPs in the, 68, 69–70, 71, 83, 95–99, 100, 162

Alaska, 138

Aldrin, 119, 163

alpha-HCH, 100, 114–15, 157, 160–62, 165, 166; half-life, 167

AMAP. *See* Arctic Monitoring and Assessment Programme

"AMAP Assessment Report, Artic Pollution Issues (1998)," 113–17, 130, 148

anemia, 137, 148–49, 151

antibiotics, 17, 18, 19

Arctic: alpha-HCH in the, 114–15, 160–62, 166; AMAP and the, 113–17, 148; aviation in the, 105, 108–9, 112; Canadian government and toxicity in the, 136; chlordane, 102, 117, 118, 135, 137, 152, 156; CINE report on the, 142, 144; climate, 106, 111–12, 123–4; disease, 111; food supply, 101, 102, 108–9, 121, 123, 136, 148; HCH, 100, 135, 136, 157, 169, 172; health problems in the, 142–43; Inuit settlement in the, 152; magazines, 155; mining, 111; oil exploration, 111; PCBs in the, 74, 92, 100–1, 114–15, 135, 137, 165, 170; pollution levels, 121; POPs in the, 101, 114, 116–17, 118, 135–36, 144, 147; settlements, 111; TDIs,

101, 110, 117, 118, 144, 155–56; toxaphene, 92, 118, 135, 137, 144, 152, 156, 162; toxicity concentration in the, 102, 121; wastewater, 107; water supplies, 107; wildlife, 114, 115, 121, 123–27, 136, 152. *See also* Baffin Island; Broughton Island; Cape Dorset; Inuit peoples; Nunavut

Arctic Basin, 136

"Arctic haze," 114, 115

Arctic Monitoring and Assessment Programme (AMAP), 103, 110, 139, 159; established, 113, 121

Arctic Ocean, 112, 136, 160–61, 166

Arctic Year, The (Freuchen and Salomomson), 126

arsenic, 119

Asia, 174, 179. *See also* China; India; Pakistan

"Assessment of Dietary Benefit/Risk in Inuit Communities: August 2000," 142

"Atmospheric Deposition of Toxics: Integrating Science and Policy" workshop, 95–99, 100

ATSDR, 167

Axel Heiberg Island, Canada, 111

Baffin Island, 117, 124, 171; POPs on, 147; terrain of, 112, 130, 152

"Beluga and Seal Fat . . . It's Good for Your Heart," 155

Bermuda, 75–76, 83, 95, 157, 162, 165

Big Rock Nuclear Power Plant, 31, 33

bioaccumulation, 42, 137, 178

biphenyl. *See* polychlorinated biphenyl

birds, 137

birth disorders, 27, 51, 84, 115, 116, 143, 148, 151

blubber, 101, 154, 156

Borlaug, Norman, 164

Boyce, Michael, 173, 174

breast milk: AMAP recommendations on, 116, 121; benefits, 137–38; contamination, 132, 134, 172; PCBs in, 74–75, 100, 121, 137–38; scare, 100, 132, 138

British Columbia: airshed, 70; and dioxin, 53

Broughton Island (Canadian Arctic): arts on, 128–29, 141, 149; chlordane levels at, 102, 138–39, 144, 147; CINE report on, 142, 144, 147, 149–52, 156; cleanup, 123, 129, 140–42, 145; climate, 130, 141; compared to other communities, 142; country foods at, 129, 130, 133, 137, 140, 142, 144, 147, 150; DDT on, 132; diet on, 147–48, 154–55; employment on, 140–41, 144; fur trade on, 141;

health problems, 133, 142–43, 145–50; Inuits on, 130, 141, 142, 144–50; medical community on, 131, 133, 145–50; mercury at, 130, 139, 147–49, 156–57; nondisclosures about food supply to, 151–52; officials of, 129, 130–31; PCB ingestion, 102, 144, 152–53; PCBs on, 74–75, 100–101, 132, 134, 137, 139–40, 147; PCB/TDI levels, 139; politics of, 141; POPs on, 137, 138, 142, 144, 147, 153, 160; POP/TDI levels, 102, 130, 138, 147–48, 153, 154; population, 130; Qikiqtarjuaq hamlet on, 129–37, 140–44, 147, 150; SAO on, 130, 133–35, 138, 139–42, 143, 144–46, 150; toxaphene on, 139, 144, 147; wastewater, 140, 141; water supply, 141–42, 144–45; wildlife on, 32, 133, 137, 152–53, 154. See also Arctic; Inuit peoples; Qikiqtarjuaq

Bush, George H. W., 34, 37, 43
Bylot Island, 117, 123–24, 126

Canada: in AMAP, 113, 137; dioxin in, 56; emissions, 69; First Nations, 31, 138; government warnings about chemicals in, 139, grain industry, 163–64; PCBs in, 75; ports, 56; TDI standards of, 156; Toronto, 66; toxaphene in, 91; water quality agreement, 63; zero discharge policy of, 32, 34. See also Arctic; Environment Canada; International Joint Commission; Inuit peoples; Nunavut
cancer, 28, 51, 116, 119, 120, 158
Cape Dorset, Nunavut, 105–8
carbon, 166
carbon-tetrachloride, 88
Carson, Rachel, 175, 178, 179
Carter, James Earl, 20
"Cause/Effect Linkages II" symposium (1991), 24, 26, 27–29, 37
cement kilns, 84–85
Center for Indigenous Peoples' Nutrition and Environment (CINE) report, 142, 144, 147, 149, 130, nondisclosure in the "Findings in Perspective" section, 151; on PCBs, 156; on POPs, 152, 156, 159; TDIs, 156; on wildlife diet toxins, 152, 153, 156
CFC. See chlorofluorocarbon
chemical manufacturing, 19
chemical spills, 179
Chemical Workers Union, 52
Chicago, Illinois, 82, 95; PCBs in, 83, 85, 86; POPs in, 96, 98
China, 89, 90, 164, 166, 178
chlordane, 70, 119; Arctic, 102, 117, 118, 135, 137, 152, 156; ban, 119, 178; Broughton Island, 102, 138–39, 144, 147; consumption of, 73, 101, 102, 152, 178; global use of, 163; half-life, 167; sources, 121, 156
chlorinated biphenyls, 76, 119. See also polychlorinated biphenyl
chlorinated organic chemicals, 118; long-term destruction, 27, 40. See also chlorine; persistent organic pollutants; polychlorinated biphenyl
Chlorinated Organic Chemicals in the Environment (Ramamoorthy), 118

chlorine, 27; banning of, 33–39, 42–44, 47–48, 61, 67, 173, 174, 175; cause/effect analysis and, 61; job loss from banning, 61; mechanism of, 50, 67–68, 166; protests against, 50; and toxaphene, 93; uses of, 38–39, 40, 50, 54. See also chlorine dioxide
Chlorine Council, 36, 37, 48
chlorine dioxide, 50–51, 53, 54. See also dioxin
chlorobenzene, 101
chlorofluorocarbon (CFC), 52, 61, 166–67
chloroform, 40
CINE report. See Center for Indigenous Peoples' Nutrition and Environment (CINE) report
"Citizen's Report Card," 57
Clean Air Act, 68, 97
cleanup: DEW Line, 75, 123, 133, 136, 140–42, 145, 153, 173; dump, 20; Great Lakes, 21, 61, 158, 159–60; paper mill, 78; PCB, 74, 81, 153; politics of, 140–42, 145; POP, 129, 176; soils, 88
Clean Water Act, 98
Clinton, Bill (William Jefferson), 43, 47, 48, 64, 74
Clinton, Hillary, 47
Clyde River, 130
Coalition of International Environmental Organizations, 49
Coberg Island, Canada, 112
Colburn, Theo, 27–28, 51, 84
cold water: Great Lakes, 92, 95; lakes in Sweden, 84, 165; toxaphene viability in, 67, 91, 162, 170; viability of POPs in, 67, 91, 100, 162, 170;
Commoner, Barry, 33–34
"Consideration of the Matter of Arctic Contaminants," 136
contaminants: airborne, 33–34, 56, 61, 66, 169–72; Arctic, 135–36; Canadian, 66–67; lake sources for, 78–79; POPs, 70, 73, 85, 168; measurement of, 58
country foods: aboriginal diet comparisons and, 142, at Broughton Island, 129, 130, 133, 137, 140, 142, 144, 147, 150; CINE report and, 144, 150, 151, 153, 156; education about, 156; Inuit preference for, 150–51; long-term supply of, 152; nondisclosures about, 151; nutritional value of, 137–38, 150; obesity and, 150–51; in Ottawa, 147; POPs in, 151, 155; raw meat, 154–54; TDIs and, 147, 153. See also Broughton Island; Center for Indigenous Peoples' Nutrition and Environment (CINE) report; Inuit peoples; Tolerable Daily Intake

DDE, 120–21
DDT. See dichloro-diphenyl-trichloroethane
Delta Institute, 95
Dene/ Métis people, 138, 142, 151
Dene Nation and Métis Association, 138, 151
Denmark, 113
Department of Indian Affairs and Northern Development, 136
DEQ. See Michigan's Department of Environmental Quality

Detroit, Michigan, 64; PCBs in, 84, 85, 87
developing nation agriculture, 89–90, 114–15, 160, 163–66, 172, 173, 176–80
DEW Line. *See* Distant Early Warning Line
dichloro-diphenyl-trichloroethane (DDT), 14, 37; Arctic, 132, 135; ban, 48, 118, 119, 120, 178; as DDE, 120–21; degradation, 120–21; global use of, 163; half-life, 167; levels, 53, 67, 119, 137; as a pure solid, 120; safety of, 118; sources, 70; TDI for, 101; toxicity of, 121; uses for, 119, 178; and wildlife damage, 23, 42–43, 118
Dieldrin, 101, 119, 163, 167
dioxin, 178; in Agent Orange, 56; airborne, 168; and birth defects, 27; concentrations, 115, 120; elimination, 50; an "illegitimate POP," 119; molecule, 120; in the paper industry, 50–51, 53–54, 55, 72, 78, 91, 93; sources of, 56, 97, 118, 119; TCDD, 120; toxicity formula, 120. *See also* chlorine dioxide
dirty-dozen persistent organic pollutants, 13, 34, 37, 118–21. *See also* persistent organic pollutants; pesticides
disease: antibiotics and, 17, 18, 19; cancer, 28, 51, 116, 119, 120, 158; diet and, 138; END, 45, 46; linked to POPs, 51; Malaria, 178; TB, 108, 111
Distant Early Warning Line (DEW Line), 75, 111, 123; cleanup, 75, 123, 133, 136–37, 140–42, 145, 153, 173
DNR. *See* Michigan's Department of Natural Resources
Donia, Robert A., 17
Dow Chemical Company, The, 22, 56, 57, 60
"Dow Shall Not Kill," 56, 57, 59

Eagle Harbor, Michigan, 73
ecosystem research, 64
Eisenhower, Dwight, 99
Ellesmere Island, Canada, 112, 135
emissions, 60, 65, 68–69, 159, 166, 169
END. *See* Exotic Newcastle Disease
endocrine disruption, 50, 51
Engler, John, 37–38, 43, 158
environmental activists, 22; against chlorine, 37, 44, 49, 50, 51, 53, 55; Commoner, 33; First Nations, 31, 56; at IJC meetings, 31–32, 49, 50, 51, 53, 55–59; locked out of meetings, 64; nuclear, 33; and POPs, 175–76; and Zero Discharge, 175
environmental compliance, 19, 20–21, 40–41, 69. *See also* Great Lakes Regional Corporate Environmental Council
environmental regulations, 21–22
Environmental Science and Technology, 99, 100
environmental sinks, 75
Environment Canada, 34, 39, 44, 48, 57, 63; atmospheric-research station, 66–67; and the POPs model errors, 163; projections, 61, 175; and toxaphene, 92; and wastewater, 108
EPA. *See* U.S. Environmental Protection Agency
Erie, Lake, 94–95

Erkkila family, 9, 25–26, 45, 71–73, 83, 127, 160–62, 163
Eskimos. *See* Inuit peoples
Exotic Newcastle Disease (END), 45, 46

farming, 89, 163–64, 178. *See* agriculture
FDA. *See* U.S. Food and Drug Administration
fines, 41
Finland, 113
First Nations, 31, 136, 138, 142, 151. *See also* Inuit peoples; Ojibwas
fishing, 25, 26; and toxicity, 28, 71–74
fish oil, 155
flourine, 166
furan, 120

gamma-HCH, 115, 161, 167
gasoline, 33–34
Germany, 113
"Global Atmospheric Behavior of Polychlorinated Biphenyls," 76
"Global Fractionation," 100
GLRCEC. *See* Great Lakes Regional Corporate Environmental Council
Gore, Al (Albert Jr.), 43, 47, 48, 84
Great Lakes: airshed, 67–68, 69–70, 83; geographical differences among, 94; POP longevity in the, 159; sediments, 80–81, 82; shoreline habitat, 65, 71–72; TDMLs, 98; toxicology, 26; water level fluctuations, 39–40; water quality, 29, 38–39; watershed, 68. *See also individual lakes by name*
Great Lakes Basin, 44, 61, 63, 64, 65; airborne POPs in the, 70; and chlorine, 33, 34, 43, 67, 175; defined, 68; eagle loss in the, 26; emissions, 60; leadership, 22, 44; paper mills, 53; PCBs in the, 114; POP spread in the, 43, 96, 175
Great Lakes Protection Fund, 65, 86, 87; Scientific Advisory Board, 66, 77, 84, 85
Great Lakes Regional Corporate Environmental Council (GLRCEC), 21–23, 68, 173; and the chlorine ban, 44–47, 67, 74; disbanded, 74
Great Lakes Water Quality Agreement (1978), 63
Green Bay, Wisconsin, 79, 80
Greenland, 113, 115, 138, 171
Greenpeace, 50
Green Revolution, 164
Grise Fiord, 112
groundwater, 40
Gulf of Mexico, 67, 68

half-life, 54, 94, 121, 167
Hamilton, Ontario, 31
hazardous substances, 40–41, 42, 43. *See also* dioxin
HCB. *See* hexachlorobenzene
HCFC, 167
HCH. *See* hexachlorocyclohexane
Health and Welfare Canada, 137
heart disease, 154, 155, 137
heavy metals, 114

heptachlor, 119, 163
hexachlorobenzene (HCB), 120, 167, 168, 169
hexachlorocyclohexane (HCH): Arctic, 100, 135, 136, 157, 169, 172; TDI levels, 101
Hites, Ronald, 75–76
Houghton, Michigan, 23–24
Huron, Lake, 84, 85, 91, 94
hydrocarbons, 69, 169

IADN, 73
ICC, 138
Iceland, 113
IJC. *See* International Joint Commission
India, 89, 164, 166
"Indigenous Women Consume Greater than Acceptable Levels of Organochlorines," 100–101
insects, 42
Integrated Atmospheric Deposition Network (IADN), 73
International Joint Commission (IJC), 28–29; chlorine ban and the, 174; and chlorine banning, 34, 35, 36–39, 43–46, 48, 49–61; and IADN, 73; 1989 Hamilton meeting, 31–32, 37, 175; 1991 Traverse City meeting, 31, 32, 35, 44, 51, 55, 157; 1993 Windsor, Ontario, meeting, 39, 47, 49–61, 63, 78, 188; and politics, 48, 63–64; Pollution Prevention policy of the, 32; 2001 Montreal meeting, 156. *See also* environmental activists
Inuit Circumpolar Conference (ICC), 138
Inuit peoples (Inuk): arts of the, 128–29, 141, 149; birth disorders of, 116; breast feeding by, 116, 138; country foods' toxicity, 121, 123, 129, 156, 172; diet, 101–2, 115, 117, 138, 152, 155–56; diet compared to Dene/Métis, 142; education lacked by, 129, 130, 156; fur trade of, 141; health problems from pollution, 115–17, 133; history of, 152; hunting by, 127–28, 152–54, 172; and the ICC, 138; language, 126, 128, 131, 141, 142; lifestyle, 106, 108, 123, 124, 126, 128, 143, 152–53; medical concerns and, 145–50; and mercury, 115–16, 117; and PCBs, 74–75, 100, 115–16; and POPs, 101, 110–11, 112, 115–17, 123, 129, 155; population, 152; raw meat diet of, 154; settlements, 111, 112; TDI levels, 101, 110, 117, 155–56; traditions, 145, 152. *See also* Center for Indigenous Peoples' Nutrition and Environment (CINE) report
Inuk. *See* Inuit peoples
Inuktitut language, 126, 128, 131, 141, 142
Iqaluit, Nunavut, 105, 107, 108, 112, 130, 145
Isle Royale, 24, 75, 165, 181
Italy, 75, 90, 93

Jacobsen, David, 28; research by, 101, 116, 144
Jacobsen, Sandra, 28; research by, 101, 116, 144
Jensen, Soren, 75, 165
Joyce Foundation, 95

Kalamazoo, Michigan (Tin City), 17–18, 19, 35, 78
Kalamazoo River, 78
Kellogg Biological Station, 42

Keweenaw Bay, Michigan, 94
Keweenaw Peninsula, Michigan, 23, 24–25

Lake Michigan Federation, 95
Lake Michigan Forum, 77–78, 81, 83
Lake Michigan Mass Balance study, 78–79, 86, 99, 159–60, 165
Lakes: Erie, 94–95; Huron, 84, 85, 91, 94; Michigan, 7, 28, 67, 76–83, 87, 91, 92, 94, 98, 101, 116, 159–60; Ontario, 91, 92, 94, 114; Siskiwit, 75; Swedish, 84, 165. *See also* Great Lakes; Superior, Lake; toxaphene
Lake Superior Basin, 26, 55, 56, 61, 66. *See also* Superior, Lake
Lake-wide Management Plan (LaMP), 77
Lansing, Michigan, 35
laws. *See* environmental regulations
lead, 119; byproducts, 33
Lindane, 115, 163, 167
lobbyists, 36–37, 38, 49, 52
London, England, 84
Ludwig, James, 24, 26, 27, 29, 42, 51, 74, 173–74
lumber industry, 26

mass-balance, 78–79, 82, 83, 86, 87, 99, 159–60
Matilda (nurse), 145–50
MCC. *See* Michigan Chemical Council
McGill University, 142
Mehan, G. Tracy, 65–66
mercury, 73, 115–16, 119, 133, 137, 148, 156–57; at Broughton Island, 130, 139, 147–49, 156–57
methanol, 40, 42
Mexico, 67, 68, 69–70, 164
Michigan: chlorine ban and, 39, 43–46; Detroit, 64; environmental issues in, 43; Governor Engler of, 37–38, 43, 158; industry and the marketplace, 55; Lansing, 35; parks, 23; PCBs in, 84, 85, 87; power plants, 31, 33, rivers, 25, 33, 40, 71 72, 78 79; Science Advisory Committee, 43–44; toxaphene in, 158. *See also* Kalamazoo; Michigan's Department of Environmental Quality; Upjohn Company
Michigan Audubon Society, 22, 45–46, 173; "Cause/ Effect Linkages II" symposium (1991), 24, 26, 27–29, 37; and GLRCEC, 44; and POPs, 23; president of the, 24, 27
Michigan Chemical Council (MCC): Government Affairs committee, 35–36; Public Affairs committee, 29; at Windsor's IJC meeting, 49
Michigan Department of Health, 158
Michigan, Lake: airshed, 76–77, 78, 80; currents, 80; DDT levels, 67; fish toxicity, 28, 101, 116; LaMP, 77; and mass balance, 81–82, 83, 159–60, 165; PCB levels, 67, 78, 80, 81; PCB sources, 78–80, 79, 82, 83, 98; POP levels, 7, 79; toxaphene in, 87, 91, 91, 92, 94. *See also* toxaphene
Michigan Manufacturers Council, 63
Michigan's Department of Environmental Quality (DEQ), 40–41

Qikiqtarjuaq (Kee-kick-TAR-yachk): co-op, 131; DDT at, 132; country foods in, 129, 130, 132, 133, 137, 140, 142, 144, 147, 150; health problems of the, 133; history, 134–35; hotel, 131, 132, 142, 143–44; nurse at, 131, 133, 145–50; officials of, 130–31, 132, 133–34; PCBs in, 74–75, 100–1, 132, 134, 137, 139–40, 147; POPs in, 130, 132, 133; SAO on, 130, 133–35, 138, 139–42, 143, 144–46, 150; wildlife, 32. *See also* Broughton Island; Inuit peoples

radioactivity, 136
Resolute, Canada, 110, 111
Russia, 178; in AMAP, 113; and PCBs, 97, 163, 165; and POPs, 96, 165; power plants in, 114

Sand Island, 74
SAO. *See* Settlement Administrative Officer
science, 43–44; and global solutions, 117; policy and research, 99
Science Advisory Committee (Michigan), 43–44
sediment, 86, 159–60, 161, 170; and PCBs, 80–81, 83, 84, 92
Settlement Administrative Officer (SAO), 130, 133–35, 138, 139–42, 143, 144–46, 150
shoreline habitat, 65, 71–72
Sierra Club, 85, 87
Silent Spring (Carson), 175
Siskiwit Lake, 75
smog, 68, 69
SOLEC. *See* State of the Lakes Ecosystem Conference
solvents, 159, 166
Spring on an Arctic Island (Scherman), 126
"State of the Health of Lake Superior," 55–66
State of the Lakes Ecosystem Conference (SOLEC): and air monitoring, 67; Detroit conference (1994), 64, 65, 66, 67; guidelines, 77; and POPs, 174
St. Lawrence River, 137
Stockholm, Sweden, 84
stratosphere, 166–67
"Studies of the Distribution of Chlorinated Hydrocarbon Pesticides and PCBs in the Arctic Ocean, 1986–1988," 135
Superfund, 20
Superior, Lake: activist demonstrations at, 55; airborne contaminants in, 56, 61, 66, 73; airshed, 114; basin, 26, 55, 56, 61, 66; bird population, 45, 180–81; cold nature of, 92, 95; condition of, 55–56, 61, 66; EPA warnings to, 158; long-term problems for, 99, 117; and mass balance, 82; PCBs in, 56, 66, 67, 75, 82, 114, 158, 165; POP longevity in, 158–60, 165; POPs in, 23–24, 26, 61, 71, 73; POP sources and, 26, 56, 61, 66, 85; pulp mill, 55; sediments, 92; toxaphene in, 87–95, 91, 117, 157–58; utilities, 55; watershed, 55; wildlife, 180; zero tolerance in, 66
Svalbard Island, 115
Sweden, 75, 84, 113, 165

TCDD (dioxin), 120
TDI. *See* Tolerable Daily Intake
"technical camphene," 121
temperature. *See* cold water
thallium, 119
"Think Basin-Wide," 56
"Think Globally and Act Locally," 175
Thunder Bay, Ontario, 55
"Tin City." *See* Kalamazoo, Michigan
TMDL, 98
Tolerable Daily Intake (TDI), 137, 151; country food, 147, 153; in Inuit, 101, 110, 117, 155–56; standards, 156
Toronto, Canada, 66
Total Maximum Daily Load (TMDL), 98
Toxaphene: advisories, 158; airborne, 89, 92, 168; Arctic, 92, 118, 135, 137, 144, 152, 156, 162; ATSDR review of, 167; banned, 89–90, 91, 92, 159, 163, 164–65, 178; on Broughton Island, 139, 144, 147; in Canada, 91; Chinese production of, 89, 90, 164, 166, 178; cold water viability of, 67, 91, 162, 170; concentration areas, 115; degradation rate of, 162, 167; in fish, 92, 115; global use, 87, 119, 163, 164; ingestion rates, 101, 118, 139, 144, 147, 152; in Italy and Europe, 75, 90, 93; Lake Erie, 94; Lake Huron, 84, 85, 91, 94; Lake Michigan, 87, 91, 91, 92, 94; Lake Ontario, 94; Lake Superior, 87–95, 91, 117, 157–58; levels, 37, 91, 91, 92, 93–94, 115, 137, 156–58, 163; mechanism of, 89, 94, 100, 121, 168–69; and PCBs, 93–94; as a POP, 42, 67, 147; in sediment, 89; sources, 70, 87, 88, 90, 92, 93, 121, 160; toxicity of, 121, 178; uses for, 88, 93, 94, 118, 119, 163; warnings omitted, 157–58; workshops, 92–93. *See also* Center for Indigenous Peoples' Nutrition and Environment (CINE) report
"Toxaphene in the Great Lakes: Concentrations, Trends and Pathways," 93
"Toxicological Profile for Chlordane," 102
Toxic Release Inventory, 60
Toxics Reduction Inventory (TRI), 57, 69, 70
toxics research, 64
"Tracking the Distribution of Persistent Organic Pollutants," 100
transport modeling, 58
Traverse City, Michigan, 23, 31, 35, 37; IJC meeting at, 31, 32, 35, 44, 51, 55, 157. *See also* Michigan Audubon Society
Traverse River, 25, 71–72
TRI. *See* Toxics Reduction Inventory
troposphere, 166, 167, 169
trout, 26, 41, 53, 54, 72, 91, 91, 137, 158

unions. *See* labor unions
United Kingdom, 113
United Nations Environmental Programme (UNEP), 89–90, 96, 98, 117, 139, 160, 162–63, 165, 176
United States: in AMAP, 113; water quality agreement, 63. *See* International Joint Commission;